D0835309

INTERCHURCH FAMILIES

INTERCHURCH FAMILIES
RESOURCES FOR ECUMENICAL HOPE

Catholic/Reformed Dialogue
in the United States

Edited by John C. Bush and Patrick R. Cooney

Westminster John Knox Press
LOUISVILLE • LONDON

United States
Conference of Catholic Bishops
WASHINGTON, D.C.

To order this publication from the U.S. Conference of Catholic Bishops, call toll-free 1-800-235-8722. In the Washington metropolitan area or from outside the United States, call 202-722-8716. Visit the U.S. bishops' Web site located at www.usccb.org.

To order this publication from Westminster John Knox Press, call toll-free 1-800-227-2872 or visit our Web site at www.wjkbooks.com.

Scripture quotations from the New Revised Standard Version of the Bible are copyright © 1989 by the Division of Christian Education of the National Council of the Churches of Christ in the U.S.A., and are used by permission.

Book design by Sharon Adams
Cover design by Cynthia Dunne

First edition
Published by Westminster John Knox Press
Louisville, Kentucky

This book is printed on acid-free paper that meets the American National Standards Institute Z39.48 standard. ∞

PRINTED IN THE UNITED STATES OF AMERICA

02 03 04 05 06 07 08 09 10 11 — 10 9 8 7 6 5 4 3 2 1

Library of Congress Cataloging-in-Publication Data

Interchurch families : resources for ecumenical hope : Catholic/Reformed dialogue in the United States / edited by John C. Bush and Patrick Cooney.— 1st ed.
    p. cm.
    Includes bibliographical references.
    ISBN 0-664-22562-4
    1. Interfaith marriage—United States. 2. Interfaith families—United States. 3. Marriage—Religious aspects—Catholic Church. 4. Marriage—Religious aspects—Reformed Church. 5. Family—Religious aspects—Catholic Church. 6. Family—Religious aspects—Reformed Church. I. Bush, John C., 1938- II. Cooney, Patrick.

HQ1031 .I568 2002
306.84'3'0973—dc21

2001051110

Contents

Preface

*T*he prayer of Jesus that "all might be one" has certainly not been fully realized in our time. We are fortunate enough, however, to live in an era in which almost all people of religion have reached out to share in conversation with others who believe in God (though they may not use that word). People of faith are reaching out to each other in order to share their personal and communal experiences of the Holy One in the most honest way they can.

Here in the United States official representatives of both the Reformed Churches and the Catholic Church have been involved in a series of six consultations with each other since the end of the Second Vatican Council. The participating Reformed Churches include the Presbyterian Church (U.S.A.), the United Church of Christ, and the Reformed Church in America. These consultations are an honest search for understanding of the various issues that are both important to our religious lives and perceived causes of our lack of unity. The purpose and goal of these six dialogues has been to search for and continue down the path toward full and visible Christian unity.

This set of dialogues began in 1965 when representatives appointed by their respective churches met to discuss and share their insights on the topics of revelation, the scriptures, and tradition. That series was very successful and fundamental to the future collaboration that occurred.

During the next thirty-six years the dialogues produced several important publications. These continue to assist members of both the Reformed and the Catholic traditions, as well as all people interested in the ecumenical enterprise. The titles of these publications are as follows:

> *Reconsiderations: Theological Conversation on Scripture, Doctrine, and Ministry* (1967)
> *The Ministry of the Church* (1970)
> *Women in the Church* (1972)
> *The Unity We Seek* (1977)
> *Ethics and the Search for Christian Unity* (1980)
> *Partners in Peace and Education* (1988)
> *Laity in the Church and in the World* (1998)

The members of this sixth and latest round of the dialogue have engaged in the endeavor with candor, honesty, and a deep respect for each other. In addressing the possibilities and challenges facing ecumenical families who seek to share their lives of faith and worship, the members of the dialogue soon realized that many (though not all) of the concerns that arise are based on language that is often misunderstood or misinterpreted. Much time was spent during the sessions trying to describe to the members' mutual satisfaction what we each believe and how we express that belief in practice. The language the participants found to express those realities has resulted in this publication: *Interchurch Families: Resources for Ecumenical Hope.*

The prime intent of the participants in this dialogue was to promote and facilitate the ongoing journey toward full, visible Christian unity. At the same time, we wished to recognize and honor those currently living in an interchurch marriage and those contemplating such a marriage. These families are at the forefront of the ecumenical experience and are a miniature of our church communities' experience of living together and struggling to make the prayer of Jesus a reality in their lives. We hope this publication will serve as a practical tool for families and for the clergy who assist them. Our efforts will have been successful if this publication helps these families and clergy in their lives and work.

The ecumenical enterprise has been and will always be the effort of both communities and individuals. We hope this publication will help us all in this most important journey to full visible unity in Christ.

Most Reverend Patrick R. Cooney, Bishop
Diocese of Gaylord
The Reverend Dr. John C. Bush
Presbyterian Church (U.S.A.)
Cochairs of the consultation

Introduction

The purpose of this sixth round of the dialogue between these three Churches of the Reformed tradition in the U.S.A. and the Catholic Church in the U.S.A. was to consider marriage and the family. The hope was to explore what these Churches have in common in their theology and practice, as well as to constructively address the issues that divide them. Members of the consultation decided to focus on Reformed/Catholic families, that is to say, families in which a member of one of the Reformed Churches enters into marital union with a Roman Catholic.

Such a union obliges the partners, their families, and their communities to consider together what is held in common regarding marriage, family life, and church practice, as well as points of difference. Without such insight and understanding, it is difficult for the partners to live their union in a shared Christian faith and to nurture a Christian family life. Those taking part in the dialogue saw such unions as an opportunity to promote mutual understanding and positive interaction between our Churches on issues of marriage, family life, and shared worship.

The chapters that follow were discussed and accepted by those named to take part in this stage of the dialogue. The introductory chapter portrays some issues and concerns facing an interchurch marriage and is thus basic to the study. The second chapter outlines what couples, pastors, and congregations need to know in order to be supportive of such unions and to integrate them into the common Christian life shared by all in our churches. Following chapters take up particular issues that are pertinent to life together and that need clarification. What the Reformed and Catholic Churches teach about marriage as a union in Christ is first presented. Then the mutual understanding and acceptance of Baptism is explained, in terms of both theology and practical consequences. This is followed by a presentation of Catholic and Reformed views of the Church, including their convergences and divergences, so that couples and pastors may have a better idea of what it means to belong in different communities and congregations and what practical matters are involved. The final chapter presents Catholic and Reformed positions on the Eucharist.

In discussing Baptism, Eucharist, marriage, and church affiliation, case studies are offered in conjunction with doctrinal and disciplinary presentations. They are intended to make the treatment more concrete and to allow readers to see the issues at stake by having them reflect on specific experiences. After reading each case, those who are using this document for group discussion might pause to ask the following: What issues are at stake? What questions need to be asked? What steps could be taken to meet the problems involved in a constructive way?

The work concludes with two appendices. The first addresses some of the practical issues that often arise, such as family planning, dispensations, and annulments. The second is a glossary of terms to help the reader understand some of the words used in the various chapters.

Chapter One

Sharing Life Together

*I*nterchurch families are a gift both for our churches and for the whole Church of Jesus Christ. The creativity and longing for a unity that can be visibly manifest, often expressed by members of such families, can serve as a witness to the whole Church. We hope that the following reflections will communicate a sense of the rich opportunities that an interchurch marriage and family can provide.

An interchurch marriage or family faces significant challenges. Questions arise, as they do for all Christians, about how to know and follow Christ within the context of one's neighborhood, work life, community, and nation. Much prayer, study, and discernment are required to sort through all the ethical and moral issues that arise, as well as to be faithful to the basic vision of humanity and the world as the object of a loving, creative, and redeeming God.

Interchurch couples and families are faced with a particular challenge. A holistic and integrated view of the Christian life seeks a continuum between personal spiritual growth and growth that takes place with one's spouse, children, friends, and fellow Christians. They are mutually interdependent, and the measure of growth in one area is often an indication of growth in other areas as well. A person's interior spiritual life cannot ignore the events of work, home, and congregational life. It is often the support of one's local congregation/parish that enables a full Christian life, but for interchurch families, the question often is, Which congregation/parish? How do spouses of different churches share Christian life together? How do the respective views of sexuality and family planning inform the marital relationship of the spouses? What about worship, religious education for the children, participation in the sacraments and other rites of the Church, service opportunities, shared study and prayer, and the other facets that inform living in Christ?

The Family

The best place to begin our consideration is the family itself. In his 1981 apostolic exhortation on The Role of the Christian Family in the Modern World,[1] John Paul II spoke of the Christian family as a community in dialogue with God. What better way to envision that smallest of communities, the Christian couple and family? The Christian family is a primary place of encounter with God.

In a very real sense ordinary and extraordinary moments of family and marital life are caught up in the life of the Spirit and become life-giving not only to spouses and children but to neighbors as well. As explained below, Catholic and Reformed Christians share both commonalities and differences in their understanding of Christian marriage. They share an understanding of marriage as a covenant in which the fidelity of the spouses to one another mirrors the fidelity of Christ to his Church. For Reformed Christians, "the essence of marriage is a covenanted commitment that has its foundation in the faithfulness of God's love."[2] While the Catholic Church affirms that it is a covenanted commitment, it adds that "the sacrament of marriage is the specific source and original means of sanctification for Christian married couples and families. It takes up again and makes specific the sanctifying grace of Baptism."[3] These theological insights provide the basis in both communities of faith for the development and nurture of marital and familial spirituality and piety.

As with many other dimensions of family life, a couple and their children discover common ways of being together, seeking to achieve a balance between work, home life, and recreation. So, too, with spirituality. In the case of an interchurch family, the spouses bring to the union their respective Catholic and Reformed ways of being Christian. Their individual experiences of participating in church life will be different, as will their personal ways of relating to God. In fact, they will discover not only diversity between the two traditions but also diversity within their own traditions as they continue to explore them. One of the rewards that many interchurch couples discover in their relationship is that they learn not only about their spouse's tradition but also more about their own.

Spirituality

The first step in sharing life together is the cultivation of a common spirituality. This will vary for different couples, but it will always include the joy and pleasure of marital relations intended to promote the self-giving, intimacy, and love of the spouses for each other. Differences among our Catholic and Reformed Churches on issues of sexual morality and family planning will need to be approached with prayer, discernment, and a well-formed conscience. These gifts and challenges of marital relationship and family planning will be an ongoing dimension of Christian life and discipleship.[4]

In addition to the spiritual dimension that is intrinsic to marriage itself, the spiritualities and pieties of their respective traditions will inform the couple's life together. There will be aspects of Catholic or Reformed life that the other partner may never entirely share. However, this does not diminish the significance of their common Baptism. Therefore, partners can find their way to each other in Christ even as they find their way to each other in mutual love. Various aspects of home and family life that have traditionally been a part of both traditions may be explored. Some of these can be revived precisely because of the challenge that an interchurch marriage poses. For example, family devotions around meals, devotions on special occasions, and even a regular time of sharing and prayer may be appropriated. Both partners bring resources out of their own traditions, or perhaps discover ways of praying that specifically reflect the family's own growing tradition. This leaves the individual partners free to continue personal prayer that reflects freedom in the Spirit and their own discipline in Christ.

Life Together

Parents are the primary religious educators of their children, if not in word then certainly by example. Though formal religious education is given in the congregation/parish, one should not forget the centrality of what takes place in the home both formally and informally. Stories from the Bible and from the lives of Christians called to be saints in both traditions should be introduced to children.

Children learn from parents what it means to live a Christian lifestyle. There will be unique challenges at every age. What basic Christian moral norms will inform attitudes toward material goods and consumer products? How will the call to simplicity in Christ inform the family's relationship to possessions, disposable income, and recreational choices? How will the Christian advocacy of social and economic justice influence civic, cultural, and political decisions and participation by the family? In an age of shifting views on sexual mores, how will conscience be shaped by a Christian vision of the human person, sexuality, and marital communion? These are but some of the issues that families and couples need to consider as they seek to live as disciples of Christ. None of these issues occurs without some relationship to the couples' respective churches and local congregations/parishes. We suggest that the faith life of an interchurch couple or family will be much more vital if it has a strong foundation in personal and home life.

While the family's religious life forms an essential foundation, equally important is their participation in the life of the local parish or congregation. This participation presents a unique set of challenges for ecumenical families. Where do members of the interchurch family worship? Separately or together? And in which church? None of these questions yields easy answers, and each family must make difficult choices as partners seek the best decision for themselves and for their children. Since Christ calls us to unity, it is not enough to remain separate, for an interchurch couple is not separate but one in their marital union. To be "ecumenical" is to discover and treasure our common faith and the continued search for Christian unity. What the family will then seek is how to live out this search in relationship to their respective churches.

We hope that families can find a way to be not only "interchurch" but also "ecumenical" for the sake of the gospel of Jesus Christ. The family partners are not the only actors in this drama. Their church communities are also involved, sometimes implicitly and at other times quite explicitly. For example, sacramental participation is considerably more open for the Reformed Christian partner than for the Catholic, who is not allowed to take Communion in a Protestant Church. This kind of input from the larger faith community may appear to be an imposition for North Americans, with their strong cultural and political traditions of individual liberty. Nevertheless, the Reformed and Catholic ecclesial traditions respect both the mandate of an informed conscience and one's responsibility to the community. After all, no one baptizes himself or herself but is baptized in the Church by its priests and ministers.

Sometimes one spouse leaves his or her tradition and joins the church of the other spouse. However, when each spouse maintains fidelity to his or her own tradition, the question arises about where to worship. Some couples may choose to worship separately in their respective churches with occasional visits to the congregations/parishes of their spouses. Others will somehow manage to attend church in the congregation/parish of their own tradition *and* that of their spouse. What we discourage is that either partner cease to practice within his or her church. The ecumenical partnership would cease if one side gives way to the other. This, of course, does not apply to those families and spouses who feel themselves particularly called to the tradition of their partner. This resource considers only those relationships that remain "interchurch" throughout marriage.

Divergences in Church Practice

Much prayer and discernment with others, including pastors, is required for a family to live in more than one congregation/parish. It is important to remember that Sunday morning does not represent the only opportunity to share in the life of the spouse's congregation/parish. Midweek services or adult studies and prayer groups, service opportunities, and socials often provide settings for rich participation. Inevitably, however, the spouses will also experience ways in which the liturgical practices of their respective traditions are different. When worshipping in two different congregations adults may find themselves disoriented by liturgical practices that are unfamiliar to them and that may evoke a feeling of "not belonging." The patterns and style of musical participation, congregational activity, and interaction within the liturgy, as well as prayer within the context of the liturgy, will vary widely between the Catholic and Reformed Church traditions. It is critical to the nurture of the interchurch marriage and family that the partners be encouraged to become familiar with the tradition of the other spouse. This is particularly important where there are parts of the liturgy that are not printed, or where there are actions that are not obvious to the "untrained" participant. It is important that the spouse from outside the tradition have these elements "accessible" in some way so as to be able to participate as fully in worship as is appropriate for his or her tradition. Conversation with the pastor and ongoing dialogue between the spouses will foster that accessibility, so that the partner from the other tradition knows not only the "what" but the "why" of the liturgical patterns. Why is the sermon so short (or long!)? Why do some churches celebrate the Eucharist/Holy Communion more often than others? Why is there more congregational/parish participation in one church and less in the other? What role does this play in the worship life of the congregation/parish? What are the theological and spiritual meanings behind how prayer is practiced?

Exploring these questions does more than simply orient one partner to the tradition of the other. In each of our traditions there is some variability, and this kind of exploration allows each partner to discuss what has shaped and formed him or her, and thereby share what is important to his or her worship life. It may be that one will never quite come to feel fully "at home" in the tradition of the other, but through conversation and increased familiarity, "different" won't always be "bad." For example, there are some forms of traditional Catholic piety (such as the rosary and other Marian devotions, veneration of the saints, sacramentals, novenas, and pilgrimages) that may be unfamiliar to Reformed Christians but that may form an integral part of the spiritual life of the Catholic spouse. It is critical that the spouses in an interchurch family share their spiritual lives so that what is important to one becomes at least familiar to the other.

The liturgical year offers its own opportunities for sharing. The central Christian mysteries of the incarnation and of the death and resurrection of Christ celebrated by all of us on Christmas and Easter will annually focus on what is at the core of shared faith and Baptism. Creatively celebrating together and perhaps even promoting joint ecumenical services involving entire congregations will enrich all involved. This is true as well for the Advent and Lenten seasons. How might the couple or family prepare together during Advent for the coming of the Lord and enter into the discipline of Lent to deepen their conversion to Christ? Such questions point to ways in which ecumenical families can lead the whole Church into deeper and richer avenues of Christian unity.

Children in an Interchurch Marriage

In an interchurch marriage the Catholic spouse promises to do all in her or his power to baptize and bring the child up in the Catholic Church. This same ecclesial obligation is not placed on the Reformed spouse, although the parental and religious concern for the child to be raised in that tradition may be just as strong. This is one point at which life for interchurch families can become especially complicated.

There are several important concerns to keep in mind. It is crucial, both for pastors and for the families themselves, that everything possible be done so that this requirement of the Catholic Church does not become a breeding ground for resentment and disaffection. It is particularly important for those in the Reformed tradition, whose churches do not impose the same ecclesial obligation, to be especially careful not to characterize the Catholic Church as the source of the problem because of the restrictions it imposes. The same attitude should hold true for the restrictions that reside with the Catholic partner and his or her church with regard to sharing the

Eucharist. In the long run, if the couple has worked through these issues prior to having children, the children will likely inherit a healthier and more positive sense of both traditions.

Children are in the formative stages of their religious development. They are usually not in a position to investigate two different churches and then choose one, so it is important for the parents to have considered these decisions well in advance of the birth of their children. It is usually best for the child to be identified as belonging in one tradition while knowing and valuing both. Christian formation, religious education, and sacramental preparation and reception should take place in only one of the respective churches. Exposure and active participation in the other parent's tradition, however, are expected and encouraged for ecumenical families. It may be possible, for example, that a child being raised as a Catholic may nevertheless attend Sunday school, vacation Bible school, or other activities in the Reformed congregation. Similarly, a child being raised in the Reformed tradition may attend worship and a variety of activities in the Catholic parish to which a parent belongs.

Parents are encouraged to baptize children in the church in which they will be raised, and though this decision can be difficult, the event of the Baptism itself can become a moment for ecumenical celebration. Because Catholic and Reformed Churches recognize each other's Baptisms, families and pastors are encouraged to invite members and leaders from the other church to attend and even to participate in the liturgy. In this way the Baptism becomes a celebratory moment in the life not only of the congregation in which it occurs but also in both of the churches that in various ways will have an important place in the life of the interchurch family.

Ecumenical Opportunities

Further opportunities for interchurch couples and families to live out their ecumenical relationships include service opportunities and participation in Christian organizations and movements. Many of these actively encourage Christians outside their church to share in their work. Local parishes and congregations may sponsor peace and justice groups, advocacy groups, and service groups who minister to the poor and address needs within the wider community. Partners may discover that their Christian lives and their marital and family relationships are tremendously enriched through Christian social activism. Ecclesial movements within the Catholic Church that are not limited to the local parish may be a fruitful place of encounter, sharing, prayer, and service for ecumenical couples. Often this entails the living out of a particular spirituality. The Taizé community—itself having a Reformed foundation—is a good example of a monastic community's reaching out to laypeople and encouraging them to a contemplative life in the midst of the world.

Many Reformed Churches sponsor summer church camps for children and youth, and these experiences, the vast majority of which include worship and prayer as a part of the curriculum, often have been profoundly influential on the spiritual life and theological understanding of the participants. In many summer church camps the population encompasses Christians of many traditions. In these settings the juxtaposition of worship, recreation, service, and witness can provide children and youth with a sense of the "wider Church" in which their own family participates in a unique way.

One of the more sensitive areas of concern that sometimes arises between our respective Churches occurs in the area of evangelization. Although the degree of emphasis varies widely within and among Christian traditions, the call to proclaim the gospel and share the good news is essential to Christian mission. All of our Churches have extensive programs of mission. A parish or congregation may launch an evangelizing effort that attempts to communicate the gospel and invite people into church membership. Those to whom this effort is addressed may be unchurched people, non-Christians, or lapsed, alienated, or former members of one's own church.

The potential for difficulty arises if the church of one of the spouses is actively proselytizing members of the other spouse's church. Our respective traditions strongly discourage such proselytism, but the possibilities of confusion in the matter may arise on the local level. Here ecumenical families and couples will have a great deal to contribute to interchurch understanding and sensitivity.

Inevitably, members of interchurch families will find themselves active in one aspect or another of their spouse's congregation/parish. It is important to be clear about one's own faith identity in this context. A Catholic in the congregation of the Reformed partner or a Reformed partner in the spouse's Catholic parish should make known his or her church affiliation to the pastoral leaders, friends, and, if possible, the entire congregation. This will alert them to the situations or circumstances where the spouse is not free to participate, as, for example, when a Catholic does not receive communion in the Reformed Church. Such openness increases sensitivity to these matters and educates everyone in a positive way. Instead of one's church affiliation being a burden when worshipping with one's spouse, it can be a blessing to all. Other Christians will benefit from or learn about the partner's tradition. It may even be possible for pastors to cooperate in developing a ritual of acceptance on the part of the spouse's congregation/parish with the full understanding that this person remains a full, active, and committed member of her or his own church. Such persons may be called on to share information about their church traditions.

Conclusion

In spite of the struggles that an interchurch family faces, it is important to end where we began: that is, with a conviction that interchurch families may present and model the hope for the eventual visible unity of the Church. For some, this may really be a matter of recognizing an ecumenical vocation as the distinct shape of one's Christian life. When ecumenical couples seek an ever-deeper response to God's love and grace, they may discover that they are particularly situated to answer Christ's prayer for unity (John 17:20). By their very relationship to each other and their presence to other Christians, they can become agents of change and promoters of Christian unity. Their love will be caught up in Christ's love for his Church. They and others with them can probe the depths and heights of the one who loved the Church and gave himself up for her in order to present to himself a glorious Church without spot or wrinkle (Eph. 5:25–27).

Chapter Two

Pastors and Congregations/Parishes

*C*ongregations/parishes to which an interchurch family relates are called by God to contribute to the development of a wholesome spiritual partnership among all concerned. This includes the family, their pastors, and the lay leadership of their respective parishes or congregations. This publication intends to facilitate that process by helping congregations/parishes and pastors take advantage of opportunities to create and maintain attitudes and programs tailored to the needs of interchurch families and their churches.

The attitudes, awareness, and ecumenical sensibilities of pastors and congregations/parishes are key to helping them contribute to the health of family relationships. In that sense, the pastoral needs of ecumenical families are not different from the needs of all families. Because of their special circumstances, however, the ability of an interchurch couple to grow in faith, understanding, and spirituality depends on three particular interactive elements:

1. The initiative and the energy the family is willing and able to put into making the interchurch aspect of their relationship work
2. The attitude and pastoral integrity of the congregations and parishes to which they relate
3. The ability and willingness of their pastors to provide them with appropriate and constructive pastoral care

What do pastors need to know and teach in order to minister effectively to interchurch families? What specific actions and programs can congregations/parishes initiate that will contribute to the health of such relationships? What attitudes and outlooks are needed to facilitate good pastoral care?

What Pastors Need to Know

Before knowing comes the awareness of not knowing. It is essential that the clergy of different churches work at the task of knowing one another and being familiar with basic elements of each other's spiritual, doctrinal, and liturgical heritage. While this basic ecumenical awareness will include some necessary study, there is no substitute for knowing each other on a personal and pastoral level in the communities in which they serve. Ministerial gatherings, even if of a purely social and apparently casual nature, have the advantage of bringing pastors together and making it possible for them to know one another at least by name and face, if not more personally. In many places, deeper opportunities present themselves in the form of ecumenical retreats, study groups, lectionary discussion groups, and community service. Pastors owe it to each other, to their congregations, and particularly to the interchurch families with whom they minister to know each other at some level and to have some basic understanding of the nature of each other's churches.[1]

The following sections discuss five essential areas in which proper understanding is needed in order for pastors to provide appropriate pastoral care to interchurch families.

Understanding the Theology of Baptism

One of the long-term benefits of ecumenical dialogue is a mutual recognition of Baptism that implies some common understanding of the sacrament.[2] Today, our Reformed and Catholic communions recognize the validity of each other's Baptism. Both Churches affirm that by the Sacrament of Holy Baptism the Holy Spirit incorporates us into Christ and joins us to Christ. For both traditions, Baptism is given once for all and is not to be repeated. Baptism signs and seals the Christian with the indelible spiritual mark of belonging to Christ. Baptism consists of washing with water (whether by immersion, pouring, or sprinkling) with the invocation of the Holy Trinity. Baptismal grace consists in the forgiveness of sin, birth to new life, adoption as a child of God, and a reception as a member of Christ's body. It is the act by which persons are incorporated into the Church, the Body of Christ, and made to share in the priesthood of Christ. Our communions baptize both children and adults, affirming that the grace of God does not presuppose any human merit.

Both Reformed and Catholic traditions appeal to the theology of the royal priesthood of the Church and its members to signify that Christian life is a call to holiness and a share in the mission of Christ and of his Church. According to early ecclesiastical writing, those baptized are anointed as prophets, priests, and kings in configuration to Christ. "Royal priesthood" was a term used to underscore the fundamental call to holiness, domination over sin when baptized into Christ, and the participation of all, as Christ's members, in the worship and mission of the Church. At the time of the Reformation, Lutheran and Reformed traditions retrieved the term "priesthood of all believers" to underscore the participation of all, not just the clergy, in the life, worship, ministry, and mission of the Church. For them, the term is always closely allied with the notion that Christ's kingship gives the baptized dominion over sin and evil. In more recent times, the doctrine of the Catholic Church speaks either of the "royal priesthood" or of "the priesthood of believers" to signify particularly the participation of the faithful in the worship and liturgy of the Church and the fundamental call to holiness of life. In addition to this, it speaks of the faithful who share in the kingship of Christ in order to express their role in the Church's mission in the world. While there are some differences in vocabulary, the Reformed and Catholic traditions both teach that the baptized are called to holiness and to take part in the mission of the Church.

Christian believers, Reformed and Catholic, are united in their Baptism. Just as interchurch couples are one in marital union, so interchurch families are one in Baptism. This affirmation provides a sacramental foundation on which interchurch families may build. It does not represent a final solution to all of the problems that such a family will encounter, but it does provide a spiritual basis and a starting point for affirming and accentuating its unity.

It is important that pastors of these two communions explore together the implications of formal baptismal affirmations for actual baptismal practice, particularly in relation to interchurch families. This would make an excellent topic to be explored jointly in local ecumenical settings. For example, when couples choose the church in which their children are to be baptized, how is the choice to be made and what participation in the sacramental ritual is open to representatives of other communions?

Understanding the Theology of the Church

Quite clearly, it is important for pastors, families, and congregations to be well informed about the understanding of the Church and of its structures on which traditions both converge and differ.[3]

When the Reformed and Catholic Churches entered into dialogue at a worldwide level, they noted that it is important for them to grasp how each tradition understands the Church, its relation to Christ, and its relation to the world. The commission for dialogue prepared and published a document on *The Presence of Christ in Church and World,*[4] which noted the witness that the Church is called to give to Christ and to God's intent to redeem the world through the sending of God's Son. The two traditions agree in speaking of the Church as the Body of Christ and on the role of the Spirit in bringing about the unity of this one body. The Church is at the service of the kingdom of God in the world and hence at the service of the world and its redemption.

The most profound difference between the churches has to do with the nature of authority in the Church. There is an extensive discussion of this matter in chapter 4 of this book. While both traditions accord a dominant place to the scriptures, in interpreting this word the Catholic Church gives an important role to the episcopacy and to the papacy. In governing the Church, the bishops and the pope are invested with an authority that is not recognized by Churches of the Reformed tradition. These matters need to be clearly explained and discussed by pastors who minister to inter-church families in order to help prevent misunderstanding and to promote deeper insight into each tradition.

In coming to a shared appreciation of the Church, the two traditions provide guidelines in their rites and orders for the Christian initiation of adults. These may serve pastors and congregations/parishes in exploring what they hold in common about the Church and its membership. There are four specific elements in this preparation that could be usefully pursued.

First is a catechesis based on the scriptures as they are proclaimed in the flow of the liturgical year. This is common to all our Churches and offers a specific format to follow in acquainting families, extended families, and congregations with the grounding of our Churches' beliefs and traditions in the scriptures and a profound sense of the Christian heritage we share in the mystery of salvation. It is in conjunction with this reading of the scriptures that congregations/parishes can be instructed in the essential teachings and precepts of their Church.

Second is Christian living, as founded in our common calling as people of God. This includes praying, bearing witness to the faith, letting the Holy Spirit inspire us to deeds of mercy and compassion, practicing the love of neighbor in tangible and practical ways, and living the moral standards we hold in common.

The third element is liturgical rites. While some sacramental practices are still barriers for us, there are many opportunities for celebrations of the Word that can unite us. These might include ecumenical celebrations such as the Week of Prayer for Christian Unity, morning and evening prayer, community observances of Thanksgiving Day, the Martin Luther King Day observance, and workshops or retreats for such practices as centering prayer and spiritual formation.

Finally, there is mission. Whatever our differences, we know that a central calling of the whole Church is to share God's good news, to build up the Church by the witness of our lives, and to profess our faith. There are significant ways we may do this together, thereby overcoming historic divisions and breaking down prejudices. It can only serve the welfare of us all and the cause of Christ when others see us working and serving together rather than living in isolation from one another.

Understanding the Theology of Eucharist

To live within the present discipline on Eucharistic sharing and to press towards fuller communion remains one of the ecumenical challenges facing our time.[5] The Decree on Ecumenism of the Second Vatican Council places this challenge within the context of our common Baptism in a way we can all affirm: Baptism is "the sacramental bond of unity" that is "ordained . . . toward a complete integration into Eucharistic communion." In that context, ongoing ecumenical conversation about Eucharist is particularly important. Meanwhile, even in our separation, we affirm that our sacramental celebration "signifies life in communion with Christ" even though we are not yet in communion with each other. We are still awaiting the hoped-for "complete integration."

Pastors need to understand both our commonalities and our differences in this regard. There are few more painful circumstances in the spiritual life of interchurch families than those faced when they come to the Eucharist. Insult and hurt feelings can easily emerge, particularly in an uninformed discussion of these issues. An understanding of Eucharist in our various traditions will enable pastors to assist their congregations/parishes, and in particular interchurch families, to develop a mutual respect for each other's theology and practice, including its possibilities and its limits.

Understanding the Theology of Marriage

A common theology of marriage is found within both traditions' understandings of marriage.[6] For both, marriage is a covenant of grace grounded in the hope of divine call and fidelity and related to the covenant and union between Christ and his Church. The primary difference concerns the sacramentality that the Catholic Church attaches to the covenant union. Practical differences are encountered on such matters as the possibilities of divorce or annulment of the union. These are areas in which pastors need to be ready to give guidance to interchurch couples.

Understanding How Couples Make an
Ecumenical Family Viable

It is not easy for a family to live in the breach between our religious communities. Deficient pastoral care can and will contribute to the instability of the family. At the same time, interchurch families can model for us what the true unity-in-diversity of the Church might be like and map out ways towards a fuller sharing.

The challenge is for churches at all levels to be intentional in helping interchurch families to share as fully as possible in church life. Do we tend to separate these families or treat them differently from others in our churches? Do we welcome them into the fellowship, mission, nurture, and worship of the church? How are their children included? How do our practices of prayer, stewardship, Bible study, and spiritual formation nurture and include them? If we do not work together to nurture the spiritual life, we risk a lack of balance in our interchurch families. This means helping them to see what they have in common as followers of Christ as well as showing them how to address the differences between their churches, as discussed in chapter 1, "Sharing Life Together."

There are several practical ways to encourage these families to participate in church life. Reading the scriptures for instruction and for spiritual nourishment is a practice common to all Christians. We also share in the rhythm of the liturgical year, the annual cycle of the mysteries of the Lord. While there may be some differences in our perceptions and celebrations of its seasons, our Churches are in substantial agreement about their spiritual and ecclesial significance.

Study of the Churches' Basic Ecumenical Documents

Pastors need to have a shared understanding of some of the Churches' basic ecumenical documents, such as the *Directory for the Application of Principles and Norms on Ecumenism* of the Vatican Secretariat for Christian Unity[7] and the document of the Faith and Order Commission of the World Council of Churches, *Baptism, Eucharist and Ministry* (BEM),[8] as well as of statements that have emerged from this series of dialogues between Reformed and

Catholic Christians. For the Reformed tradition, importance should be given to the various Lutheran and Reformed agreements as well, for these provide essential insights to some of the issues involved.[9]

Our church life does not exist in a vacuum, nor are any of our churches merely local congregations or parishes. Each of our communions is part of a larger group, though the structures of church government are remarkably different. In addition, each of us understands and affirms the ecumenical nature of the Church. The modern ecumenical movement formally began after 1910 with the World Missionary Conference at Edinburgh and blossomed over the following decades. The reforms of the Second Vatican Council thrust the Catholic Church into the mainstream of this movement. The result has been a plethora of ecumenical opportunities for dialogue, research, understanding, and mission. The series of Catholic-Reformed consultations out of which this publication has emerged is but one example of the ways our churches have sought to make our unity in Christ more visible.

It is neither necessary nor desirable for local clergy and lay leaders to reinvent the ecumenical wheel in seeking to understand and address the questions and challenges presented by interchurch families. A vast store of theological and pastoral insight is available from various approved and received documents, representing a remarkable level of consensus and agreement. Basic awareness of such documentation and knowledge of how to access it as need arises will serve pastors and religious leaders well.

What Congregations Need to Know

It is not enough, however, for clergy involved in ministry to interchurch families to educate themselves. Congregations and parishes should also be educated about how they contribute to the spiritual health and stability of these families. While such education must have the active support and encouragement of the clergy, lay leadership can carry out much of the hands-on effort. This includes those who are responsible for parish education, worship, spiritual nurture, and catechesis.

In our congregational and parish settings we can provide a context of acceptance and comfort through constructive attitudes. It is crucial that congregations/parishes be what they profess to be: communities of grace, love, and fellowship. God's people are especially equipped to mediate the liberating grace of God; to become sustaining, supportive communities of faith; and to strengthen one another in mutuality and faith.[10]

In the communities where we live and work side by side, it is essential that we seek opportunities for the Reformed and Catholic communities to know each other and work together in a variety of ways. Possibilities include shared study of the scriptures, community service, joint food pantries, and ecumenical prayer services. Recent developments in liturgical renewal have resulted in worship resources that seek to recover some of our shared liturgical traditions. These developments present a new array of ecumenical worship opportunities through Services of the Word, morning or evening prayer, and other forms of common prayer on a variety of occasions.

Of particular importance for our concerns here would be jointly sponsored support groups for interchurch families. The American Association of Interchurch Families and its international manifestation present a model for such an approach. Guidance and assistance in this regard are also available in a book by Father George Kilcourse, *Double Belonging: Interchurch Families and Christian Unity.*[11]

Conclusion: An Understanding Attitude

Good pastoral care can be provided by both clergy and lay leadership in parishes and congregations. It should be based on an attitude of respect, a desire to support people's faith life, a commitment to support ecumenical families, and an openness to bringing families together to discuss their strengths and difficulties. All of us must undertake this task with appropriate humility as we seek to understand and recognize our often divisive past. Both Reformed and Catholic Christians have inherited a tradition of bias, prejudice, and exclusivity in regard to each other, even as we have remained in our respective ways faithful to the gospel of Jesus Christ.

Positive attitudes in our communities can have lasting effects that reach far beyond the needs of particular families. Such attitudes can and should develop into multiple opportunities for our Churches to come together regularly for ecumenical prayer and common service. In the end, all of us must find ways to support the ecumenical endeavor.

Chapter Three

Our Common Baptism

*I*n 1990 the second phase of the Reformed/Catholic International Dialogue declared that "our churches should give expression to mutual recognition of Baptism. [This recognition] is to be understood as an expression of the profound communion that Jesus Christ himself establishes among his disciples and which no human failure can ever destroy."[1] The growing presence of interchurch families makes such expression particularly urgent. Although the mutual recognition of Baptism is hardly denied among Reformed and Catholic Christians, making this theological understanding a lived reality among the faithful is another matter. While all Christians face this dilemma, interchurch families live in the midst of this struggle in ways that are particularly difficult but also instructive. Their experiences are a reminder not only that disunity matters but also that claiming the gift of our existing unity liturgically and pastorally matters as well.

To make this presentation of more practical use, comments are included on a particular case that is then woven into the enunciation of doctrinal and ecumenical considerations.

The Case: Where to Baptize Ryan

David, a member of the United Church of Christ, and Bernadette, a Catholic, found little difficulty participating fully in their respective Christian traditions while honoring one another's faith community. They both attended worship in their own congregation/parish and participated in their

mission, education programs, and social activities while still find-
ing regular opportunities to attend and participate in the celebrations of their partner's church. Except for the inability to take
eucharistic communion together, this interchurch family experienced little stress in leading its religious life. This all changed,
however, with the birth of their first child, Ryan. Immediately the
question confronting Bernadette and David, as well as their
extended families, was, "Where will Ryan be baptized?" The
choice to be married in a Catholic parish seemed "natural" in a culture where weddings traditionally take place in the bride's church,
as this one had. David's pastor had been included in appropriate
ways, and both families felt good about this ecumenical experience. Deciding where to have Ryan baptized, however, challenged
the limits of the ecumenical commitment of each of their families.
In this case the culture offered no guidance. To choose one church
seemed inevitably to upset the careful balance both David and
Bernadette had worked hard to achieve. One church, and therefore
one extended family, would "win" while another would "lose."

The Counter Demands of Culture

Such notions of "winning" and "losing" are not surprising in the
context of a culture marked by patterns of belonging shaped by the
spirit of voluntary association. We belong to and leave groups,
organizations, associations, communities, and even families on the
basis of our own free choice. These patterns of belonging are rein-
forced by a prevailing individualism and are complemented by key
elements of our capitalistic economy: consumerism and competition. When belonging is determined by individual free choice,
when membership or nonmembership is based on personal decision, groups find themselves competing for the allegiance, loyalty,
and participation of potential members. Thus, fraternities and
sororities "rush," colleges or the military "recruit," and civic organizations develop marketing strategies. Members become con-
sumers. In a highly mobile society, this phenomenon is intensified
to the point where even our primary community of affection is

determined more often by the friends or colleagues we choose than by our extended family of origin.

This cultural reality has profoundly influenced the shape of ecclesial life in North America. It contributes to a religious landscape that is markedly different from the state churches of Western Europe (whether Catholic or Protestant); or the interpenetration of religion, nationalism and culture in Orthodoxy; or the influence of family, community, and tribe in many parts of Asia, Africa, and the Pacific. While it may have provided strength and vitality to North American ecclesial life, it has also had a significant negative impact, leading to serious misunderstanding and distortion. In addition, it has obscured the given unity of the Church and sometimes led to a weakening of the ecumenical impulse. When belonging is seen as the result of voluntarily "joining a church" rather than of being incorporated into the Body of Christ, it is not hard to understand why "church shopping" becomes a prominent feature of contemporary church life. If personal choice is the primary factor in determining church membership, it is not hard to see why North American churches—particularly Protestant churches, though not exclusively so—are so rigidly divided along lines of race, class, or ethnicity, a fact demonstrated over sixty years ago by H. Richard Niebuhr.[2]

Such a state of affairs has a particularly corrosive effect on ecumenical families like that of David and Bernadette. Parents and grandparents, church members, and even spouses are left wondering why "their church" was chosen over "our church." Suspicions of "unfair competition" may even be harbored when the "choice" is between churches whose canonical requirements offer greater or lesser flexibility in response to "consumer needs." To be sure, the crude analogy of the marketplace is seldom used overtly, but its influence is pervasive.

Baptism in Ecumenical Dialogue

The theology of Baptism in recent ecumenical convergence documents and the mutual recognition of Baptism assumed throughout most of western Christianity offer a profound challenge and corrective to this state of affairs. One might even say that by virtue of its mutual recognition, Baptism could be "countercultural" in North America, challenging notions of membership and belonging that rely on market models and that reduce the understanding of "Church" to narrowly local expressions. This declaration from *Baptism, Eucharist and Ministry* is the fundamental starting point:

> Administered in obedience to our Lord, baptism is a sign and seal of our common discipleship. Through baptism, Christians are brought into union with Christ, with each other and with the Church of every time and place. Our common baptism, which unites us to Christ in faith, is thus a basic bond of unity.[3]

Recent Catholic reflections on Baptism use similar language, reminding us that Baptism orients the individual toward community and away from any private or parochial understanding of faith. In the *Directory for the Application of Principles and Norms on Ecumenism,* the *koinonia* established in Baptism is intimately related to the eucharistic communion that is its goal. The Church becomes not merely the community of those who have chosen to join it through the ritual of Baptism but the communion of those incorporated by the Holy Spirit through Baptism into the Paschal Mystery: the life, death, and resurrection of Christ.

> Baptism . . . constitutes the sacramental bond of unity existing among all who through it are reborn. Baptism, of itself, is the beginning, for it is directed towards the acquiring of fullness of life in Christ. It is thus ordered to the profession of faith, to the full integration into the economy of salvation, and to Eucharistic communion.[4]

Something far more than personal choice, individual initiative, and the attractiveness of a local congregation or parish are involved in Baptism and Church membership. Our belonging, at its core, reflects and reveals the choice and initiative of God and has to do with universal rather than exclusively local participation.

The baptismal rites of most churches incorporate this understanding. The Roman Rite of Baptism for Children testifies that through baptism men and women are incorporated into Christ. They are formed into God's people, and they obtain forgiveness of all their sins. They are raised from their natural human condition to the dignity of adopted children. They become a new creation through water and the Holy Spirit. Hence they are called, and are indeed, the children of God.[5]

The United Church of Christ's *Book of Worship* states that "a person is incorporated in the universal church, the body of Christ, through the sacrament of baptism." This fact is implicitly, if not explicitly, named in the blessing that follows the Baptism itself: "The Holy Spirit be upon you, child of God, disciple of Christ, member of the church." In the Reformed Church in America, the declaration and welcome that follows the Baptism states that the baptized is "received into the visible membership of the holy catholic church." In the Presbyterian Church (U.S.A.) the rite affirms that the baptized has been "received into the one holy catholic and apostolic church through baptism. God has made them members of the household of God."

Baptism *signifies* and *effects* a membership and belonging radically at odds with the personal choice, competition, and extreme localism inherent in the practice of voluntary association at the heart of North American culture. A recent study document of the Lutheran World Federation points to the ecclesiological implications:

> Baptism reflects a fundamental aspect of the church as communion. The church is not self-constituting. Its fundamental character is given to it by God. The church is thus a dependent reality, dependent upon the institution of its essential actions by Christ and upon the activity of the Spirit within these actions. We receive the communion which the church is. . . . The *given* character of baptism points to the church as a communion in Christ and thus precisely a communion under Christ's lordship.[6]

In other words, Baptism challenges North American Christians to think about their "ecclesiastical landscape" in very different ways. Churches—or denominations—are not isolated and distinct organizations competing with each other for members in the fashion of the Rotary and Kiwanis clubs. Again, in the words of the Lutheran study document,

> a recognition of our baptismal unity should undercut the false ecumenical solution of a comfortable denominationalism in which the churches each tend their own gardens, careful not to bother or insult others, but in no way living out or even seeking a truly common life.[7]

Just as there can be no truly "isolated Christian," there can be no isolated church. "A church that chooses isolation is a church in self-contradiction."[8] Regardless of the church in which it is celebrated, no Baptism can be viewed with indifference by other churches. Whenever a person is baptized, he or she is brought into some kind of communion, however imperfect, with every other church by virtue of the mutual recognition of Baptism. When someone is baptized at Covenant Presbyterian Church, the membership of St. Anne's Catholic Church a block away is somehow enriched. How unlike our normal conditions of accounting, in which profit in one place requires loss in another! As the Roman rite reminds those who are to be baptized, "The Christian community welcomes you with great joy. In its name, I claim you for Christ our Savior by the sign of the cross." Implied in this statement is the presumption that the joy being experienced extends far beyond existing denominational boundaries.

This is not to suggest that it is a matter of no significance where a person is baptized. One is never baptized by the universal Church but always by a particular church, normally by an ordained minister recognized and authorized to perform the sacrament in that local church (whether defined as denomination, communion, diocese, or congregation). Baptism implies a responsibility for care and nurture that is in some sense unique to that particular church. The person being baptized will exercise his or her ministry and discipleship within a particular community of faith. Baptism does not wash away distinctive traditions, confessions, or practices. But this truth is always relativized by the underlying truth that baptism *by* a particular church is always baptism *into* the universal Church.

Practical Concerns

The capacity of Baptism to signify the unity of the Church is largely dependent on, and may often be diminished by, the church's practice. Much can be done either to enhance or to obscure Baptism's ecumenical significance. One issue that can render Baptism's ecumenical impact ambiguous is the lack of clarity about the relationship between Baptism and church membership. While all would agree that Baptism makes one a member of the Body of Christ, different churches have differing understandings of when and how a person becomes a member of a particular congregation. Often this is related to Confirmation or to First Communion. If one sees these "moments" as marking different stages of membership or even different forms of membership, the separation of Baptism from Eucharist and confirmation (at least for children) in the Western church can undermine the unity given in Baptism. This is especially true if "full membership" is conferred in separate rites with separate understandings at a later point in a person's life. If the membership given in Baptism is either implicitly or explicitly understood in the community as being somehow contingent on later confirmation, then the baptismal unity may also be made contingent.

By restoring the Rite of Christian Initiation of Adults in the early seventies, Catholics have tried to heal this historical separation in their own Western Church, now manifesting the original practice of the Church in maintaining the unity of the sacraments of initiation. This restoration raises questions about the current practice of the initiation of children (and even of infants) and promotes extensive dialogue among pastoral leaders regarding the isolated reception of the Sacrament of Confirmation. The restoration of the catechumenate has not only become a teaching moment for Catholic assemblies, but it has also brought to their awareness the theology of initiation and the power of the unity of the three sacraments that bring about this initiation. As these revised rites help to restore the relationship of Baptism in the full paschal mystery expressed through the Eucharist, care needs to be taken that these rites celebrated for candidates seeking full communion with the Catholic

Church do not have the unintended effect of calling into question the Baptism that has taken place in another ecclesial tradition at an earlier point in the candidate's life. In the United Church of Christ service of "Reception of Members: Affirmation of Baptism" (the name of this service itself reveals the ambiguity to which we have been referring), the following prayer seeks to address this concern:

By your baptism you were made one with us in the body of Christ, the church. Today we rejoice in your pilgrimage of faith which has brought you to this time and place. We give thanks for every community of faith that has been your spiritual home, and we celebrate your presence in this household of faith.[9]

A second kind of problem arises with those who practice the Baptism of adults only on personal profession of faith. This practice may result in the inability to recognize the Baptism of infants or young children. Beyond this, there are churches that do not baptize in the name of the triune God, and still other churches that do not baptize at all. While none of these latter situations applies directly to the relationship of Catholic and Reformed Churches, "nonrecognition" existing within the universal Church is a grave obstacle to the ecumenical implications of the sacrament.

A third concern arises because this universal sacrament is most often celebrated in denominational or even congregational or parish isolation. The faithful rarely "see" the ecumenical reality being signified. Of help is the fact that more and more baptismal rites share a common order, use common creedal affirmations, and employ similar baptismal prayers. (However, experimentation with the language of the traditional baptismal formula in many denominations may become a challenge to recognition.) The practice of having "ecumenical witnesses" at baptismal services can do much to make the ecumenical significance of Baptism visible. Ecumenical services "commemorating" or "affirming" our common Baptism can also highlight the implications of Baptism for the unity of the Church. In the *Directory for the Application of Principles and Norms on Ecumenism*, we read,

According to the local situation, and as occasion may arise, Catholics may, in common celebration with other Christians, commemorate the baptism which unites them by renewing the engagement to undertake a full Christian life which they have assumed in the promises of their baptism, and by pledging to cooperate with the grace of the Holy Spirit in striving to heal the divisions which exist among Christians.[10]

Of course, the most profound obstacle to the full appropriation of the ecumenical meaning of Baptism is the inability of churches that have mutually recognized each other's Baptisms to enjoy a full Eucharistic fellowship or to reconcile fully their ministries. A Lutheran World Federation publication poses the troubling question:

> If Lutherans, Baptists, Catholic, and Orthodox all truly baptize (a not insignificant "If"), then they all baptize into, and thus in some sense belong to, the one church of Jesus Christ. If we then cannot live out that unity in a common life of worship and mission, something is deeply wrong. How can we be one, yet not one?"[11]

This fundamental contradiction is a stark reminder of the anomaly of our divisions. If we greet this contradiction with acquiescence, then one can justifiably call into question the integrity of our baptismal unity. If, however, it becomes the source of urgency for Christians who "share a real though partial communion" to work for greater unity, then the anomaly may be of significant service to the ecumenical pilgrimage.

Ryan's Baptism

Ryan's Baptism took place in Bernadette's Catholic parish, but it was not an easy decision. Though sensitive to David's church involvement, Bernadette felt bound to the promise about the religious upbringing of children she had made to her church at the time of their wedding. David felt great commitment to his church, but he was not required to make a comparable promise. While he knew that other people made different decisions, it became apparent that he personally could accept the Baptism of his child at the Catholic Church more comfortably than Bernadette could accept the Baptism at the United Church of Christ. David's pastor, his family, and many of his friends from the United Church of Christ attended the baptismal liturgy. One week later, during the morning worship service in the United Church of Christ, Ryan's baptism was "recognized" by his U.C.C. family. Care was taken that the ritual created for the occasion was clearly not a second baptism. The words of the ritual called the congregation to rejoice in the baptism *that had already taken place* at Bernadette's church—a baptism that had significance for David's church as well. In the ritual of recognition, David, Bernadette, and Ryan gathered at the front of the sanctuary, away from the font. Water was not used, further emphasizing that this was not a rebaptism. The congregation pledged its support for Ryan, accepted its responsibility for his Christian nurture, and acknowledged that this responsibility would be carried out with Bernadette's parish. The faith of David's family was celebrated as part of Ryan's shared inheritance. Finally, Bernadette's family was invited to share in the service of recognition, and her pastor was consulted to ensure that the precise nature of the celebration was understood and affirmed by all.

These two liturgies—the Baptism itself and the service of recognition celebrated one week later—helped to dramatize the mutual recognition of our common Baptism. Both families and both congregations were helped to understand that Ryan's Baptism was God's choice and God's reception of Ryan into the universal Church, rather than simply a choice by his parents for or against a particular ecclesial tradition. Both families and both local churches were challenged to consider the meaning and implications of a sacrament celebrated within a divided Church. Together, the two liturgies *represented* the ecumenical reality of a common Baptism and *helped to create* that reality.

This celebration will not be the last time David and Bernadette face the challenges of a divided Church. Christian nurture, confirmation, attendance at worship, and above all, the inability to share together at the Eucharist will be issues of enduring challenge for this family. But rituals express and help to create a reality. We hope that the reality of our common Baptism, dramatized by the two liturgies celebrating that event, will continue to inform and shape the way this family addresses ongoing challenges. As one liturgical scholar reminds us, "The moment we discover the potential power in the liturgical consensus already granted us—and begin to act on it—is the moment many other things will fall into place. . . . Sacraments are not just theological concepts, but the gospel in action."[12]

Conclusion

The countercultural aspect of the Sacrament of Baptism has important theological, pastoral, and vocational implications for ecumenical families. If the meaning of Baptism is fully claimed theologically, and if it is appropriated in the teaching, liturgical practice, and pastoral care offered by the churches, then ecumenical families will be relieved of the burden of needing to choose between differing churches and, by extension, of choosing between family members loyal to those churches. Congregations will be relieved of the burden of competing for loyalty, members, and the participation of members who are part of ecumenical families. Instead, they will be encouraged to engage in an ecumenical collaboration that nurtures the faith, life, and witness of those ecumenical families regardless of which church is the site of the Baptism or the arena for the exercise of their discipleship.

Seen within the context of a unity rooted in Baptism, ecumenical families can visibly embody the gift and the call of unity. Even the occasion of eucharistic division, so painful for these families, can become the call to live their ecumenical vocation. In their Baptism and at the Table, ecumenical families make visible in a unique and compelling fashion the reality that "we are one, and yet we are not one." Rather than choosing to be representatives of competing and irreconcilable groups, ecumenical families, by virtue of their Baptism, are members of one Body, reconciled in Christ, but as yet unable to express its unity. They become for the wider community of faith a constant reminder, a gentle encourager, and a judge.

As one observer of the phenomenon of interchurch families expressed it, spouses and children who strive to live the unity of baptism and marriage personify necessarily the nagging questions for the divided churches. . . . They pose the embarrassing question: Are the churches allergic to the possibilities for unity which the Holy Spirit offers us?[13]

In a context even broader than the individual interchurch family, all of us are challenged to see that

a recognition of our unity in baptism should be a spur that reminds us of the inherent anomaly of divided churches. As call, our baptismal unity should move us to ecumenical engagement. As gift, however, our baptismal unity should give our ecumenical engagement confidence.[14]

Chapter Four

The Church

Its Ministry and Its Authority

As ecumenical families seek to share their life and their faith together, many of the situations that require thought and conversation have to do with how each of the partners thinks about the church tradition to which the other belongs. For example, in moral matters Reformed and Catholic traditions have different ideas about how the authority of the Church relates to the authority of the gospel. In ministerial matters, they differ in the ways in which ministry is passed on and in what is thought to be the range of an ordained minister's activities. In this chapter, the major questions that occur about the Church are briefly treated. A case illustrates some of the issues at stake. This is followed by a summary of the ways these two traditions have now reached ecumenical convergence, overcoming many of the mutual suspicions engendered by the history of division. After that, the Reformed and Catholic positions on key matters are explained. Finally, a word is said about the mutual recognition of the Churches and their ministries, the extent of this recognition, and its limits.

The Case: A Not-So-Friendly Visit

Bernard, a Presbyterian, and Sandra, a Catholic, had been married ten years. Their three children had been baptized in the Catholic Church and were all in Catholic schools. Once, when they were sure they did not wish to risk having another child, they had used contraceptives for a period of time, but generally Bernard respected Sandra's desire to abide by the

Catholic teaching on family planning. On Sundays, each attended service in the congregation/parish of their own Baptism. Once a month, Bernard accompanied Sandra and the children to the Catholic parish and then the family went on to worship in the Presbyterian church. Neither received communion in the other's church. When the Presbyterian congregation welcomed a woman, Pastor Henrietta, as its minister, Sandra felt somewhat uncomfortable with the service but nonetheless stuck to her side of the couple's mutual understanding.

Then Margaret, an old friend of Sandra, came to stay for a few days. Her visit coincided with the Sunday when Sandra went to the Presbyterian church, so Margaret went with her and Bernard and their children after all had been to Mass. When they came out of the service, Margaret took Sandra aside and remarked, "I don't know why you keep going there; that woman is not even a priest, and they only ape the Catholic Mass without really knowing what they are doing." This upset Sandra quite a bit, and after Margaret had left, she decided it was time for her and Bernard to pay one of their occasional visits to her parish priest, Father Henry.

Father Henry explained that it was true that the Catholic Church did not allow the ordination of women and it also has a different understanding of orders than the Presbyterian Church. For one thing, the Presbyterian Church does not have bishops, and Catholics believe that bishops belong to the ministry as it comes from the time of the apostles. For another thing, the ministry of the Presbyterian Church is passed along outside the structures of the apostolic succession of bishops. All the same, he could not countenance Margaret's comment about "aping the Catholic Mass." As he put it, when Presbyterians come together for Holy Communion, they gather in faith to celebrate Christ's death and resurrection. They also believe in the gift that Christ makes of himself to his people. Father Henry did not know quite how to express what is done. He did, however, quote the Vatican Council on the presence of Christ and the Spirit in the Eucharist of churches whose ministries the Catholic Church sees as authentic and genuine ministries of the gospel, though it views them as somehow incomplete.

After this, Bernard and Sandra thought a visit to Pastor Henrietta in order. She explained to them that the Presbyterian Church, like other Reformed Churches, acknowledges the change in its structures that occurred with the Reformation, including a change in the way ministry is handed on. However, all these churches believe that in the interests of the proper preaching of the Word and the proper celebration of Holy Communion or Lord's Supper as Christ had wished it celebrated, this break had been necessary. She also took down from her shelf the *Book of Common Worship* of the Presbyterian Church and the *Sacramentary* of the Catholic Church and pointed out how close the two services are to one another, though there are some notable differences. The similarities and differences did not mean, she noted, that one is "aping" the other, but that both churches have revised their liturgies with a like faith about the Eucharist in mind and in an effort to renew the liturgy in keeping with ancient tradition and the New Testament. In the end, Pastor Henrietta, like Father Henry, advised Sandra and Bernard to continue as they had been doing, respecting the faith and the celebration of both communities. Neither pastor was sure how and when difficulties about ministry would be sorted out, but they felt that in the meantime the best way forward was with respect and understanding for the practice of both the Presbyterian and the Catholic Church.

Ecumenical Convergence

Churches of the Reformed tradition and the Catholic Church share the confession that the Church is rooted in God's election of Israel as well as founded in the passion, death, and resurrection of Christ and the proclamation of the gospel. In this, all our churches profess that the existence of the Church on earth comes forth from within the Trinity. The Father has sent his Son and his Spirit into the world to save humankind from sin, to make of us a new creation, and to call us to be witnesses to the truth of the gospel.

The professions of faith that we have in common express a shared belief that the Church is the Body of Christ and the dwelling place of the Spirit. In its visible reality, the Church of today is one with the apostolic church. It seeks to maintain the faith taught by the apostles who were the eyewitnesses to the life, death, and resurrection of Christ and who first proclaimed the forgiveness of sins through his saving power.

Our churches also share the confession that believers and disciples are united together into one communion through the preaching of the Word and the celebration of the sacraments of Baptism and Eucharist. In recent ecumenical literature, the word *koinonia* (or communion) is often used to designate this oneness. It reflects our communion in the life of the Trinity, our communion in one faith and in charity, as well as the need for the visible elements of community that hold a body together and make it a witness to Christ in the world.

This broad outline must here suffice to name the belief in the Church and the conviction of being Church by God's gracious call. Given this common sense of what it is to be Christian, couples joined in interchurch marriages can find it hard to grasp what holds our Churches apart, especially when it comes to the celebration of the sacraments. The following paragraphs explain the differences between our Churches so that the issues faced may be more comprehensible to all.

Reformed Teaching

A Reformed View of the Universality of the Church

While both the Catholic Church and Churches of the Reformed tradition share much in common regarding our love and loyalty to the Church of Jesus Christ, each tradition emphasizes unique themes. It is our hope and prayer that these themes will finally complement each other and help to offer to God and the world a more faithful community of service.

For the Churches of the Reformed tradition, the essential marks of the Church (that is, the catholicity of the Church) are found in the worship life and ministry of the local congregation. This is where Reformed Christians believe human beings experience the reality of the mystical Body of Christ most directly. They affirm that the Church is present wherever the Word of God is faithfully preached and the sacraments of Baptism and Eucharist faithfully celebrated within a congregation that is mutually caring and accountable. The gathering of a particular community of faith around Word and Sacrament is at the very heart of a Reformed understanding of the nature of the Church.

However, this picture of the catholicity of the Church should not be understood in a narrow or parochial way. As has already been explained, those who are baptized in both the Catholic and Reformed Churches are received, first and foremost, into the universal Church, the Body of Christ, the household of God. This reception into the Church catholic is realized as the baptized are received into a particular congregation where they will be nurtured in the faith. The Sacrament of Eucharist is also understood within the Reformed Churches as a sacrament that must be available and offered freely to all baptized Christians. And so, although both sacraments are celebrated in a local church, they are meant for the growth of the whole Church. The catholicity of the Church can thus be most clearly seen as a local congregation gathers around the Word of God and celebrates the Sacraments of Baptism and Eucharist.

In addition to these essential marks of the Church, the Churches of the Reformed tradition also embrace the ecumenical creeds (Apostles' and Nicene) as historic and faithful witnesses to the Word of God, defining the classic marks of the Church as "one, holy, catholic and apostolic." The ecumenical councils of the Church have helped clarify a common understanding of the faith that inspires our journey toward the oneness Christ has promised us.

Finally, it is essential to understand the offices of the Church with which reside the responsibility to serve Christ in both congregational life and in the world. The offices of the Church serve first the local community of faith and are called to nurture a common life of hope, faith, and love. These offices (or orders as they are called in other Christian traditions) are a gift from God to assist congregations to form their life around Word and sacraments. The minister of Word and Sacrament, often called the pastor, is examined and ordained by a gathering of congregations and there-fore held in love and discipline within the larger Church. Just as the worship and beliefs of the Reformed Churches reflect the Church catholic, so the offices of the church, especially the office of minister of the Word and Sacrament, are intended to serve the whole body of Christ as well as the world. And so, with the whole Church, Reformed Christians joyfully confess "one, holy, catholic and apostolic Church," and embrace all churches marked by the faithful preaching of God's Word and celebration of the sacra-ments of Baptism and Eucharist.

A Reformed Understanding of Apostolicity

With other Christians, the Reformed Churches confess faith in "one, holy, catholic and apostolic Church." Where is the sign of apostolicity found among Reformed Christians? First it is impor-tant to say clearly where it is *not* sought or found. It is not in an unbroken lineage of bishops tracing their ordination back to the apostles and to Jesus Christ himself. The term "apostolic succes-sion" is known in Reformed circles only through ecumenical dia-logue with those Christian communities who make such a claim.

The mark of apostolicity is manifested in faithfulness to the apostolic witness to "the faith once delivered to the saints." Reformed Churches stand, along with other Christian churches including Catholic ones, in the succession of those who have pro-fessed their faith in Jesus Christ as Divine Savior and Lord and have sought to follow him in repentance and Baptism and serve him in the world. It is the faith of Peter when he confessed, "You are the Messiah, the Son of the living God" (Matt. 16:16), to which Reformed Christians are committed, rather than to Peter himself or his successors.

Within this understanding, the Reformed practices of ordination consist of prayer, with the laying on of hands by those who have been similarly ordained. This historic practice is significant to a Reformed doctrine of ordination but in itself does not either sig-nify or convey apostolicity. Rather, it is continuity with the apos-tolic witness that is signified. Neither this nor any other rite can guarantee, convey, or represent a direct succession from or to the first disciples or their successors.

In Reformed teaching the priesthood consists of all baptized believers. Thus, the title "priest" refers to this universal priesthood, not to a particular office or order. It is called "universal" because all believers participate in it through their Baptism, having been joined to Christ the High Priest who "remains the only priest forever" (Second Helvetic Confession). In Reformed understanding, there is no special office or order whose prerogative it is to offer a sacrifice of propitiation, since Christ's high-priestly sacrifice on the cross is sufficient in itself. Thus, the universal priesthood of all believers is grounded in the sacrifice of Christ himself. This evangelical sufficiency is at the heart of the apostolic faith that all Christians confess.

The Reformed concept of *priesthood* is different from the office or order of *ministry* that derives from it. As the Second Helvetic Confession says, "The priesthood . . . is common to all Christians; not so is the ministry." The office of ministry is one of function and therefore is not sacramental. The ordained ministry acts on behalf of the whole community, representing and facilitating the ministry of the whole. This ministry consists in the public proclamation of the Word of God, which includes the functions of teaching, preaching, and administering the sacraments of Baptism and the Eucharist. Because it is a representative ministry of the whole community, women as well as men may be ordained to it. Because the ministry is communal in nature, the communities are in communion with each other but not necessarily with a particular minister. The local (and universal) churches are in communion with each other based in their common Baptism, and for them eucharistic hospitality may rightly be a means to as well as an expression of Christian unity.

Ordinarily, the sacraments take place only in the presence of the gathered, worshipping community, not as private celebrations. The Eucharist is to be made available explicitly to all the baptized, even though some who are present may not be in a position to accept the invitation. Such eucharistic hospitality derives, as we have seen, from an essential element in contemporary Reformed ecclesiology.

Catholic Teaching

Within the horizon of common belief and profession given above, the Catholic Church offers specific teaching as to how the Church is constituted as God's people and the Body of Christ.

In the first place it believes and teaches that the apostolic tradition of the Church in life and faith, already noted as a common tenet of our Churches, is guaranteed by the apostolic succession of its bishops. What this means about the passing on of order and ministry is that the rite of laying-on of hands must be done in a succession that remains unbroken from the time of the apostles. This ritual of sacramental succession was in fact broken at the time of the Reformation. The Reformed Churches, in order to keep alive the ministry of Word and Sacrament within themselves, instituted and installed their own ministers without keeping this tradition. They placed themselves outside the communion of churches that acknowledge the primacy of the See of Rome. While the Catholic Church now accepts these as true ministries of Word and worship, it believes that unless reconciled with the Catholic communion through acknowledgement of the primacy of the Bishop of Rome and a laying-on of hands, there is something lacking in them. This is because, in the eyes of the Catholic Church, they have not kept a constitutional element of the Church as a body that dates back to the apostles.

The Catholic Church also believes that ordained ministry is a sacrament and that it is made up of three offices: the episcopacy, the presbyterate (often called the priesthood), and the diaconate. Churches that have not kept the episcopal order are not seen as in full conformity with apostolic tradition. This is because the Catholic Church believes that Christ willed the pope, as Bishop of Rome, to have primacy of teaching and government in the universal Church. While the whole Church is embodied in every local church (that is, *diocese*), each of these local churches (*dioceses*) needs to be in communion with the Bishop of Rome in order to be fully a part of the universal Church.

In ecumenical dialogue with other Christian churches, such as the Churches of the Reformed tradition, the Catholic Church has come to acknowledge in them specific embodiments of the Church of Christ. In order to express its recognition of the ecclesiality of other church bodies, while at the same time maintaining that only the Catholic Church has all those characteristics intended by Christ for his Body, the Second Vatican Council taught that "the Church of Christ subsists in the Catholic Church, governed by the successor of Peter and bishops in communion with him." At the same time, it recognizes that many elements of the Church and its sanctifying ministry are found in other bodies, in which Christ and the Spirit are present and active.

The role of the baptized faithful in the life and mission of the Church was affirmed at the Vatican Council and continues to be developed to this day. The way in which the Council showed the connection between the role of the ordained and the role of the laity was to relate them both to Christ—priest, prophet, and king. It could then show how both the faithful and the ordained, each in their distinct but respective ways, have a share in this threefold office of Christ, sent by the Father to call all the redeemed into his Body and to bring salvation to the whole world. In teaching about the nature of Christ's Church, the Catholic Church sees that sacraments are a necessary constituent of this Body and presents an understanding of their nature and number. This teaching proved problematic and divisive at the time of the Reformation, and it is now a topic of continued ecumenical dialogue.

The foundation of the teaching on sacraments is the vision of the Church itself as "sacrament or sign and instrument of the intimate communion with God and of the unity of the whole human race."[1] In numbering the sacraments, the Church includes seven rites. Besides the two primary sacraments of Baptism and Eucharist, it names five others, each intended for a specific purpose in the life of the faithful and of the community of the Church. These are Confirmation, Matrimony, Holy Orders, Penance, and the Anointing of the Sick. Each of these is a statement and realization of the life of Christ and the Spirit in the faithful and their communities. They are seen as particular manifestations and realizations of the life and reality of the Church itself as sacrament of Christ, living in a visible way in the midst of the world, infused with and making known the invisible and active presence of Christ and the Spirit.

The sacramentality of these rites is imbedded in a larger sense of the sacramentality of creation. This Catholic understanding differs from a Reformed understanding of the sacred nature of all creation. Despite original sin and a creation flawed by human fault, Catholics are persuaded that finite creatures still express the wonder and glory of God. They are the fruit of God's self-giving that transcends them completely but brings them into communion with the divine. Hence, in the sacraments, bread, wine, oil, water, and light show forth the life and wonder of the world and of the human being, have a divine significance, and are suffused by divine life. It is on this account that when Christ came to redeem the world, he took up creatures of the earth and integrated them into the mystery of his incarnation and into the proclamation of his mystery of salvation. Even now, within his Church, he continues to be present among his followers and continues to sanctify them by joining the words of his gospel to these creatures. In the conjunction of word, creaturely element, and ritual, the sacraments are the signs and the efficacious action of Christ's grace, in and through the ministry of his Church.

While there is much more to the teaching of the Catholic Church on Christ's Body,[2] these appear to be the points of doctrine that need to be kept in mind and clarified in the course of ecumenical conversations and for the sake of interchurch families. From the case presented, it can be seen how they affect the relations of a couple and their congregations. Sandra was upset by Margaret's comments on the ministry of the Presbyterian pastor. She and Bernard had to work out their position on family planning, keeping in mind the claims of the teaching of Catholic Church authority. Sandra's participation in the liturgy of her husband's Church was on the one hand affirmed and on the other restricted because of the way in which the Catholic Church looks on the ministry and on the communion of the Church. In the course of their married life, Bernard may experience tension every time that his wife or his children seek out one or other of the "other five" sacraments. Views on the sacramentality of creation and on the use of tangible objects in devotion that readily go with the Catholic view on the nature of sacrament are certainly matters that affect the way in which a couple share their devotional life.

The Mutual Recognition
of Churches and Ministries

In recognizing the Baptisms celebrated in one another's Churches, Catholic and Reformed Churches recognize that we all belong in some way as communities to the Church, the Body of Christ. We see each other as communities in which the Word of God is proclaimed, faith in the gospel is embraced, Baptism and the Eucharist are celebrated, and Christ and his Spirit are actively present. We see each other also as communities with which we share the mission of giving the witness of Christ to the world. At the same time, as the case study painfully illustrates, the Churches of the Reformed tradition and the Catholic Church struggle with the form and history of each other's ministries. For the Reformed Churches it may seem that the Catholic Church allows its understanding of episcopal order to prevail over the right teaching of the Word of God and the right administration of the sacraments of Baptism and Eucharist. While accepting that the sacraments of the Eucharist and Baptism are celebrated in the Catholic Church, Reformed Christians are concerned that both these and preaching can be overpowered by Catholic positions on ministry and on the teaching authority of the magisterium in interpreting the Word.

The Catholic Church for its part finds deficiencies in the ministry of the Reformed Churches for two reasons. First, it views the ministry of Reformed Churches as being outside the line of ritual apostolic succession. Second, it views them as lacking the full communion with the Bishop of Rome. The Reformed Churches concur with these two points but, of course, do not identify them as deficiencies.

While the Vatican Council says that "the Church of Christ subsists in" the Catholic Church, it speaks of other bodies either as churches or as "ecclesial communities." This last term is left deliberately vague. On the one hand, it serves to designate a body such as the World Alliance of Reformed Churches, which does not see itself as a church but which fosters communion among churches and exercises an ecumenical mission. On the other hand, the phrase serves to distinguish within the Body of Christ between the Catholic Church and other bodies. In the eyes of the Catholic Church, those other bodies lack some of the orders and ministries that belong to the Church's constitution but whose relationship to the Body of Christ the Catholic Church nonetheless wishes to recognize.

While the Reformed Churches would allow their members to receive eucharistic communion in the Catholic Church, the Catholic Church is not able to reciprocate. This is because the Catholic Church believes that sharing the Eucharist is the sacramental expression of full communion that supposes the ministerial and structural unity of communion among the bishops of the Catholic Church.

Hence there is a genuine recognition of ordained ministries along with some quite significant reservations. Each Church sees the ministry of the other as an answer to a call of Christ and the Holy Spirit. Each sees the other's ministry as a means of communicating the Word of God and the life of Christ and the Spirit. The Catholic Church is more hesitant about the words used in expressing its views about the celebration of the Eucharist in Reformed Churches, but it does see it as the celebration of Christ's passion, death, and resurrection and as a sign of the effective presence of Christ and Holy Spirit.[3]

We all affirm and believe that God's Word is passed on and that Christ and his Spirit are actively present in other communities as well as in our own. The communion in Christ and the Spirit celebrated in Baptism runs deeper than the problems aroused by teaching on the Church and the practice of ministry. Nevertheless, considerable theological and structural convergance will be required before we can give full recognition to one another. In the meantime, much interchange and sharing is possible on the basis of the recognition already achieved and in the hope of a further progress.

Chapter Five

The Covenant of Marriage

While a marriage between two Christians of different religious traditions may be recognized by both Churches as a holy union, there are both convergences and differences in what the Reformed and Catholic traditions teach about this union. As a guide to couples and their pastors, these teachings are reviewed in this chapter within the context of current ecumenical interaction and dialogue. The theological presentation is preceded by a case study in order to make the discussion more concrete.

Case Study: Where to Marry

Catherine and Mark waited nervously for their appointment with Catherine's pastor, Bob. They had met and fallen in love at school and now wanted to marry. They were very happy but knew that they had to face the question and problem raised by the fact that Catherine was an active and devout Presbyterian and Mark was an active and devout Catholic. The interchurch match had caused some stir of gossip in Catherine's small Texas town where suspicion between Catholics and Reformed Christians remained. Now they hoped that somehow Catherine's pastor could help them plan their wedding in a manner that would honor both their traditions and help them understand how they could both maintain those traditions and grow together as a couple in Christian love.

Catherine's pastor was helpful. Reformed Christians understand marriage as a covenant, he said. That is similar to the Catholic position, but Catholics also understand marriage as one of seven sacraments instituted by Christ. Pastor Bob suggested a future meeting with the Catholic priest they had invited to witness their marriage because he wanted to be sure that Catherine grasped the Catholic understanding of marriage as clearly as Mark understood the Reformed position. He was also eager to help the couple plan a wedding that would mark the beginning of a strong marriage. The couple had told Pastor Bob they had struggled with their faith as they thought about marriage. They had discussed marriage in either of their churches or even the possibility of being married in a church of a third denomination. Ultimately they decided that they wished to be married in a church of one of their own traditions. In the course of their conversations they began to realize that they each wished to be faithful to their own church traditions and that for Mark it was important to remain a full communicant member of the Catholic Church.

Catherine was delighted to learn that she could indeed be married in the church where she had been baptized and raised. Mark was excited that the Catholic Church would recognize the marriage there as sacramental. There were some specific steps they needed to follow for this to happen, in which they had the informed guidance of both pastor and priest.

This is what they learned: Reformed Christians recognize the validity of marriages performed by other clergy. The Catholic Church, on the other hand, has a requirement that the marriage of a Catholic must ordinarily be celebrated before a priest or deacon and two witnesses in order for the marriage to be considered as a sacramentally valid marriage. The requirements of the Catholic Church for a marriage to be considered *sacramental* are that marriage be entered into as a life-long commitment, that the spouses express intent to remain faithful to one another,[1] and that they be open to the possibility of having children. When they discussed these characteristics of marriage with Pastor Bob, he indicated that although the Presbyterian Church allows divorce and remarriage in extenuating circumstances, it nevertheless understands marriage to be permanent and presumes that the couple will remain faithful to one another. Although Reformed Christians understand children to be a gift of marriage, there is no requirement that the couple necessarily be open to the possibility of having children.

The priest explained to the couple that while the Catholic Church certainly recognized other marriages as *civil* unions, the Catholic Church also recognizes them as *sacramental* when they meet the conditions set down in the canon law of the Catholic Church. Canon law, he added, makes special mention of the fact that, for those who are not Catholic, observance of Catholic ritual is not expected. Father Tom then told them that Catherine and Mark could request from the bishop a dispensation from the requirement that a Catholic priest or deacon or other delegated person witness a marriage in which one or both partners are Catholic.[2] The marriage could then take place in Catherine's church and be officially witnessed by her minister.

The couple also had the choice of having the marriage at the Catholic Church and inviting Catherine's pastor to assist. They decided to have the marriage at the Presbyterian Church, but they did want Father Tom to be present and participate in the marriage ceremony. The priest was helpful in guiding the couple through the process of applying for the dispensation. Catherine's pastor cooperated in making sure that the necessary paperwork was done. It really helped to have both clergy cooperating. Of course, one of the clergy might have contacted the other by phone and negotiated the details, but it meant a great deal to the couple that both clergy actively participated in the preparations.

The couple continued to meet with both members of the clergy as they planned their wedding. Catherine's pastor addressed the difficulties and challenges that lay ahead for Mark and Catherine as an interchurch couple. He helped them think through their practices of worship and Bible study. He asked them about children and where they might be baptized and raised. He spoke to them honestly about the inevitable difficulties in raising the children in the church of one parent while the other parent worshiped in another setting. But Father Tom also talked about the rich traditions of both churches, and how he imagined they could more fully appreciate and learn from each other's tradition. He spoke frankly to them about the pain involved in not being able to share in the Eucharist.

He urged Catherine and Mark to be persistent in the coming years as they worked out unexpected difficulties. Their growth together as a Christian couple could model unity to others and show that it is possible to raise children in a home with one Catholic and one Reformed parent.

The couple arranged several meetings with Pastor Bob for their premarital counseling. They also met with Father Tom for Catholic marriage preparation. Both Father Tom and Pastor Bob emphasized that a couple preparing for an interchurch marriage should be prepared for marriage in both traditions. Mark and Catherine filed the Premarital Investigation (PMI) in the Catholic tradition. Father Tom explained that while the name sometimes varies from diocese to diocese, the basic purpose of the PMI is the same. Namely, it seeks to determine that each party is free to marry in the eyes of the Catholic Church, that the couple understands the nature of Christian marriage, and that they intend to contract a marriage that is sacramentally valid in the eyes of the Church. When Mark and Catherine met with Father Tom to complete the investigation, Mark brought copies of his baptismal, first communion, and confirmation certificates with him; Catherine brought her baptismal certificate.

Father Tom made sure that the couple understood that in order for the dispensation for the marriage to be granted, Mark must be asked to reaffirm his faith as a Catholic. He must also promise to continue the practice of that faith, especially by doing his best to have any children of the marriage baptized and raised as Catholics. Father Tom was careful to point out that Mark's promise was to be made in the context of Catherine's conscience as a Reformed Christian. Mark could either sign a written promise or make it orally in front of Father Tom. They spent a long time discussing the promise and asked many questions. Father Tom told them that Mark had an obligation to respect Catherine's conscience when their children were born. He stressed that no decision as important as the Baptism and Christian education of children should be made by only one parent. Father Tom made sure that Catherine was comfortable with the decision for Mark to make the promise, because he knew that Reformed Christians sometimes have concerns about that promise. Mark made the promise, and Father Tom requested the dispensation from the bishop for the marriage to occur at the Presbyterian Church with Pastor Bob officiating.

Father Tom then made arrangements for the couple to attend one of the marriage preparation programs required by the diocese. He explained that the program would help them engage spiritual and emotional questions important for the strength of the coming marriage. These meetings are often held over one or more days to prepare couples for marriage and are especially helpful for those entering into an interchurch marriage.

Mark and Catherine then met with Pastor Bob to plan the actual wedding ceremony. He reviewed the service with them and showed them places where they could select prayers, scripture readings, hymns, and music, with some elements also drawn from the Catholic marriage liturgy. They also discussed the possibility of the celebration of the Eucharist since both Catherine and Mark had expressed a desire to celebrate the Eucharist during the wedding. In the end they decided not to do this, feeling that it was not pastorally sensitive either to the couple or to their families and guests. They learned that if the wedding were taking place in the Catholic Church, Catherine might receive permission to take Communion during the wedding ceremony. However, this permission would be for her alone and would not apply to family members or guests who were not Catholic. They also learned that although Mark would be welcome to receive communion in keeping with Reformed practice, he would not be permitted to do so under Catholic church law.

They did note the many ways in which the liturgies of both Churches are similar. They agreed which prayers and readings they would ask Father Tom to do. Pastor Bob, as the presiding minister, would witness the marriage vows. The couple asked a Catholic friend to be a lay reader and met with the organist to select music for the ceremony.

Mark and Catherine's wedding was a wonderful celebration marking the beginning of their marriage. They had made their journey together with a greater awareness both of the possibilities and potential difficulties of their spiritual life together, but they were also equipped to think through concerns and seek solutions that honored both traditions. Such a beginning is a strong foundation on which a couple can chart a course for Christian growth.

Ecumenical Convergence

In their respective liturgies, the Catholic Church and Reformed Churches relate marriage to the doctrine of creation and to the doctrine of redemption. They seek to bring the marriages of the baptized into accord with the will of God and to allow the marriage relationship to be patterned on the covenant of Christ with his Church and of God with God's people. Hence they celebrate marriage as a covenant and a commitment to discipleship in this way of life.

Addressing the issue of mixed marriages, an international Lutheran-Reformed-Catholic Commission (1976)[3] underlines the fact that two Christians who approach their union in faith are united in marriage on the ground of their common Baptism. The covenant of God with the world as its creative source is given an unsurpassable expression and fulfilment in the covenant of God with Israel and in Christ's spousal relationship to the Church. The baptized join together in marriage as a way of living this covenant that has its origins in God's love, knowing that the relationship of Christ to the conjugal life of Christians confirms it with the promise of his grace. While Catholics call this covenantal union a sacrament, Reformed Churches choose not to use this title because they find no scriptural warrant for it and hold to the unique place in the life of the Church of the sacraments of Baptism and Eucharist.

Reformed Perspectives
on Marriage as Sacred Covenant

The Reformed Churches understand Christian marriage as a sacred covenant into which the partners are called by God and within which they give themselves freely to one another. It is not seen as a sacrament of the Church. The couple, together with their family and friends, gather in the presence of God to witness the joining together in which two become one flesh. They surround them with prayers and seek God's blessing upon them. Finally, they pledge the support of the community of faith as the couple seeks to live out their love for one another. In this way the new couple is strengthened for their new life in a nurturing covenant community, the Church. Ordinarily, the marriage ceremony occurs in the place of worship and within a ceremony based on the Service for the Lord's Day. Its form may be either a Service of the Word or a eucharistic celebration.

The idea of marriage as covenant is based on scripture, in which the Lord enters into covenant with God's people and calls them into covenant with God and with one another. The first such covenant is the covenant of creation in which God created human beings male and female. God gives us to one another for mutual help and comfort, to live in fidelity to one another "in plenty and in want, in joy and in sorrow, in sickness and in health, throughout all their days."

The covenant of marriage is intended for the full expression of love between the couple who now belong together and who freely give themselves to each other with tenderness and affection. This self-giving, mutual bond embodies the essence of covenant.

There are several God-given purposes of the covenant of marriage. Among these are the well-being of the whole human family, the proper ordering of family life, and the birth and nurture of children.

For Reformed Christians, as for Catholic Christians, marriage is a holy mystery in which the two are joined together and become one, just as Christ is one with the Church. It calls the couple to a new way of life that is created, ordered, and blessed by God and that is entered into with a sense of prayerful responsibility.

With Catholics, the Reformed Churches affirm that Christian marriage is marked by permanence and fidelity. Unlike the Catholic Church, however, they do not hold that an openness to bear children is intrinsic to the nature of the covenant. No legal forms of contraception are proscribed by these Churches, though abortion as a means of birth control is specifically not condoned. Divorce is confessed to be a sign of human failure and sin but does not constitute a barrier to remarriage in the church. However, in the course of human events there will inevitably be times when vows exchanged in all sincerity and with the best of intentions are not or cannot be kept by one or both parties. Sometimes, as the Westminster Confession of Faith acknowledges, "marriage dies at the heart and the union becomes intolerable."[4] In such cases, Reformed and Presbyterian Churches permit separation or divorce.

In no event, however, is such permission taken lightly. Again, the Westminster Confession of Faith recognizes that "the corruption of man [sic] is apt unduly to put asunder those whom God hath joined together in marriage" and affirms that the Church is concerned "with the present penitence as well as the past innocence or guilt of those whose marriage has been broken."[5] Just as such a break

> . . . may occasion divorce, so remarriage after a divorce granted on grounds explicitly stated in Scripture or implicit in the gospel of Christ may be sanctioned in keeping with his redemptive gospel, when sufficient penitence for sin and failure is evident, and a firm purpose of and endeavor after Christian marriage is manifest.[6]

In the best of circumstances, divorce represents failed intentions and is a reflection of human sinfulness. The covenant of marriage has been broken, and this reality has consequences for both parties, for their children and extended families, and for the community of faith. None of this is taken lightly, and it calls forth expressions of pastoral care and concern for all of those involved in and affected by it. The Reformed Churches also affirm, however, that "nothing can separate us from the love of God" and that the ministry of the church is and must continue to be fully available to those caught in such circumstances.

The Book of Worship of the United Church of Christ provides an "Order for Recognition of the End of Marriage." This service is "intended for those occasions when a couple has experienced a divorce and wishes to acknowledge responsibility for their separation, affirm the good that continues from the previous relationship, and promise in the presence of God, family, and supportive friends to begin a new relationship." The service is penitential in nature and "cannot be construed to be an encouragement of divorce or a deprecation of marriage."

Churches in the Reformed tradition hold the reality of the inevitable dissolution of some marriages in tension with the understanding of the sacred nature of the marriage covenant. They recognize that in all of life's circumstances Christians continue in the baptismal assurance that "nothing in life or in death shall be able to separate us from the love of God in Christ Jesus our Lord."

For Reformed and Catholic Christians alike, then, marriage is a powerful symbol of God's faithfulness, love, and grace freely given and received. It is a part of Christian discipleship as Christians live out their baptismal faith. The life of fidelity and forgiveness that marriage requires models the very essence of what it means to live as one in Christ.

Summary of Catholic
Teaching on Marriage

While the differences on this question are not as sharp as in the sixteenth century, there are specifics to Catholic teaching that need to be noted.[7]

Marriage as Sacrament

When the Catholic Church calls marriage a sacrament, several points are included in this teaching. The marriage union that was established by God in creation under the old covenant became a sign of the fidelity of the divine covenant with the people of Israel. In the dispensation of the New Testament in Christ, it is a sign of the bond between Christ and his Body, the Church, and a state to which the grace of Christ is assured. It is not a justifying sacrament, that is one intended to take away sin (as are Baptism and Penance), but as a sacrament for the baptized it carries with it an assurance of grace to live the married state faithfully and as disciples of Christ.

It is the couple themselves who are the ministers of the sacrament, and in this celebration they exercise the royal priesthood of the baptized, itself a participation in the priesthood of Christ. According to Catholic teaching, the ritual of the Sacrament of Matrimony is located essentially and principally in the exchange of consent between the couple. In giving their consent to their marital union and pledging themselves to each other, they also express their agreement to the purposes of marriage, which are mutual love, life-long fidelity, and the bearing of children. The ceremony incorporates other appropriate symbols that fit within a culture, such as the exchange of rings and the joining of hands or the placing of a veil over the couple, and is allied with a proclamation of the Word, a blessing over the couple, and celebration of the Eucharist.

Since it is a share in the mystery of Christ and of the Church, entry into marriage is to be witnessed by the Church within an appropriate and officially recognized ritual, and it is necessarily related to the Eucharist in which the partners partake as a couple. The official witness to this entry into marriage is normally an ordained minister but not necessarily so, and hence the Church's law allows for the rare occasion when marriage may be officially witnessed by any baptized member of the Catholic Church. Ideally the entire service takes place in the presence of the gathered community.

Entered into in this solemn fashion, the marriage union is a holy estate, to be lived in fulfilment of baptismal justice and commitment, and a union in which persons are sanctified by fidelity to Christ and to the ordinances of God regarding marriage. In virtue of its sacramental celebration, it carries with it an assurance of grace to live the married state faithfully and as disciples of Christ.

Consequences

In Catholic doctrine and practice, the following consequences are drawn from the sacramentality of marriage. A valid marriage is one that is celebrated according to the prescriptions of law and ritual and that is not impeded in any way by church law. Every valid marriage of the baptized is a sacrament because of the fundamental baptismal consecration and discipleship of the couple, which places their marriage within the order of the new covenant. Hence canon law considers as sacramental any marriage properly entered into by two validly baptized Christians, whether they be Catholic or members of other Christian churches.

As for the qualities of the marital sacramental union, it is monogamous and indissoluble, to the complete exclusion of divorce. However, allowance is made for dealing with difficult situations.[8]

Conclusion

This chapter has shown the extent to which an engaged couple needs to understand what it is to marry as Christians from two different church traditions. They can find agreement and mutual love in fundamental perceptions that are drawn from the scriptures. They will also, however, realize that within this common faith perspective there are differences as to the sacramental nature and purposes of marriage. Working through this to a mutual understanding and covenant inspired by faith in Christ belongs to marriage preparation, but there are other times during married life when these matters need to be freshly taken into account.

Chapter Six

The Eucharist

This chapter reviews the doctrine and practice of the Eucharist in relation to the lives of interchurch families. After a case study that highlights the difficulties faced, a word will be said about approaches to the Eucharist in current ecumenical dialogue. This discussion will be followed by a brief review of Catholic and Reformed teaching.

Case Study: Joined and Separated in Desire for the Eucharist

It was March 19, three days before Teddy was to receive his First Communion at St. John's Catholic Church. The family had prepared for this day for a long time. Teddy's parents, Janet and Bill, had taken part in the parent preparation classes at the parish, and everything seemed ready. However, as the day drew closer, Bill was increasingly uncomfortable. From the early stages of their relationship, even while they were still dating, Bill and Janet had discussed what their future might be like when they married: blending families, balancing career and family, where they might live and work. And, of course, since Janet was a Catholic and Bill was an active member of the United Church of Christ, they had prayerfully discussed in which church they would marry.

At the time of their engagement, the couple decided it would be helpful if they attended one another's church occasionally to help them understand the tradition in which each had been raised. What seemed like a great idea became the first major tension in the relationship. The first week, Janet decided that she would accompany Bill to his church. In preparation, Bill had described the worship service and shared some of the Church's teachings about the Eucharist. He informed Janet that his Church had an "open table," allowing others who were not members of the United Church of Christ to receive Communion. Janet had been a little uncomfortable even about attending Sunday worship with Bill, so she spoke with her pastor who encouraged her to do so since the two of them seemed to be moving toward a more serious relationship. However, he reminded her that Catholic Church discipline did not allow her to receive Communion in Bill's Church. He then reviewed the Catholic Church's teaching on the Eucharist and the lack of unity between the Churches, and encouraged her to enter into the prayer but not to fully participate by receiving Communion. He also reminded Janet that, under usual circumstances, Bill would also not be able to receive Communion when he joined her for Mass.

Janet didn't want to start out their efforts on a negative note, so she didn't discuss the matter but simply accompanied Bill to church, joined in the prayer and song, but did not receive Communion. Bill didn't quite understand why she didn't receive the sacrament, but he didn't pressure her and felt that eventually she would do so when she became more comfortable.

The next week, when Bill was scheduled to join Janet for Mass at her parish, the issue had to be faced directly. In helping to prepare Bill for what he would experience on Sunday, Janet explained the outline of the Mass and when he was to stand and sit, and then told him that he would not be able to receive Communion. After struggling with an explanation, she handed him one of the worship aids from the parish that had some printed guidelines about receiving Communion. The guidelines had a section for Catholics and one for "Fellow Christians" that began with a word of welcome and a reminder about our common Baptism and the work of the Spirit in drawing Christians together in the Eucharist. So far, so good. However, the second paragraph stated that because Catholics believe that the celebration of the Eucharist is a sign of the reality of the oneness of faith, life, and worship, members of those Churches with whom the Catholic Church is not yet fully united are ordinarily not admitted to Holy Communion. The paragraph went on to talk about exceptional circumstances and special permissions and special groups. The next paragraph encouraged those not receiving Holy Communion to express in their hearts a prayerful desire for unity with the Lord Jesus and with one another.

Bill read the paragraph several times before starting the discussion again. While he had known that various Churches had different positions on theological questions, he thought the ecumenical movement had brought them to a greater level of unity. In fact, he knew that the Leuenberg formula of agreement for "full communion" among the Lutheran and Reformed Churches clearly recognized each Church as one in which the gospel is rightly preached and the sacraments rightly administered. While there was not complete theological consensus about the Lord's Supper, there was mutual recognition of and allowance for members to receive Communion in each other's churches. He had realized that this was not the case with the Catholic Church, but when he was affected by it, it just didn't seem right. It was one thing for Janet to be invited to the Table and to choose not to receive. It was another for him to want to receive and to be told that he could not. And from Janet's explanation it seemed that this might be the case for most of their married life. Both took their spiritual life seriously, and this was a roadblock in their relationship, one that neither of them had anticipated.

When Bill accompanied Janet to Mass, he sat alone in the pew as she went forward to Communion. Though he respected her Church's discipline and belief, the experience was painful. As she knelt beside him, she sensed his pain and frustration. The next week they decided that they would worship separately, each in his/her own Church. However, while the tension over receiving Communion was absent, so was their experience of worshiping together. The next week, in an attempt to resolve the tension and to explore what this reality might mean for their future, the two of them met with both pastors.

Each pastor was understanding and helpful, but also honest. An ecumenical family lives daily with the lack of unity between the

Churches and experiences the pain of separation in a personal way. Bill's pastor explained gently and carefully the implications of the agreement on full communion with the other Churches and the policy on the open Table and spoke respectfully of the different position taken by the Catholic Church. If two people loved each other and wanted to grow together spiritually, there would be ways to find unity, but it would not be easy. Janet listened carefully, thinking about the future and what this might mean eventually for their spiritual life and for the children who could be "caught" between two Churches.

After the meeting at the United Church of Christ, the couple met with Janet's pastor. He spoke about the Eucharist as a source and a sign of unity, and about the painful lack of unity between the Churches both in faith, church law, and practice. And he reiterated the importance of authentic signs and symbols of unity in Christ and the need to find occasions and elements of faith that they might share as well as the need to continue to treasure their own traditions and the differences. While not wanting to minimize the difference in practice, he also spoke about the few occasions when Bill might be able to receive Communion in the Catholic Church. The bishop could permit this on their wedding day, perhaps for a child's First Communion, or for a funeral. But the same would not be true for Janet. Catholic directives simply prohibited her from receiving Communion in the United Church of Christ due to divergent understandings of ordination and the Eucharist itself.

That was eight years ago. Now Janet and Bill face the questions once again as they consider Teddy's First Communion, and they will continue to do so on similar occasions throughout their life together.

This case study illustrates the problems and the pain that can arise around the reception of the Eucharist. That a couple is encouraged to go together to a eucharistic service in either Church shows that there is a measure of respect for what is done there and some common faith about its meaning. That they cannot receive Communion together obliges them to inquire into the eucharistic faith of both their Churches. How can a split that occurred almost five centuries ago over the Mass or Lord's Supper still have such

repercussions in church discipline and in church life in this ecumenical era?

Eucharist in Ecumenical Dialogue

Reviewing the disputes of the Reformation era in historical perspective and taking current approaches into account, the Reformed
and Catholic communions in recent decades have found considerable convergence in their doctrine and celebration of the Eucharist.
Together, they recognize a biblical basis to the historical celebration
of the Eucharist in Christian churches. They look to the foundation
of such celebration in the practice of the Lord's Supper in the prim-
itive Church, in what Jesus did at his Last Supper with his disciples,
and in the background of the Jewish Passover, which is known to us
from study of the Bible and complementary texts of Jewish tradition. The actions and words of Jesus at the Last Supper, expressing
his willing acceptance of death and his gift to his disciples in love
and obedience, inaugurate the new covenant in which God's
promises to Israel are newly operative. From the beginning, Christian communities gathered together with glad and generous hearts to
celebrate the memorial of the death and resurrection of the Lord in
the sharing of the one loaf and the one cup. In this way, they experienced the presence of the risen and exalted Lord in his Church, in
virtue of his once-for-all sacrifice and by the power of his Spirit.

In the gift of bread and wine that are blessed, and over which
the words of Jesus are pronounced, Reformed and Catholic
Churches recognize the gift that Christ makes of himself to his
people in this sacramental manner. They also find in the eucharistic celebration a living and effective memorial of the death of the
Lord, the once-for-all sacrifice that he made to the Father for the
forgiveness of sins. In this way, the mystery of the Church united
in the Eucharist is a living communion with the risen and glorified
Christ, of whom it is the Body. It is a foretaste of the heavenly ban-
quet for which we all long.

The presence of Christ in the Eucharist is the work of the Spirit,
whose sending is invoked in prayer and effected through the signs

of the bread and wine that are shared at the common Table. It is on the specific manner of this presence, and on the specific nature of the Eucharist as memorial and sacrifice, that the Churches differ in their explanations.

Current Catholic Teaching
on the Eucharist

The current teaching of the Catholic Church on the Eucharist is based on this paragraph of the Constitution on the Liturgy of the Second Vatican Council (no. 47):

> At the eschatological supper, on the night he was being betrayed, our Saviour inaugurated the eucharistic sacrifice of his death, by which the sacrifice of Christ might be perpetuated until he would come, and in this way he could entrust to the Church, his beloved spouse, the memorial of his death and resurrection. This is a sacrament of mercy and faithfulness, a sign of unity, a bond of charity, a paschal table fellowship, in which Christ is consumed, the mind is filled with grace, and a pledge of future glory is given to us.

On the institution of the Eucharist at the Last Supper, the *Catechism of the Catholic Church* says:

> The Lord, having loved those who were his own, loved them to the end. Knowing that the hour had come to leave the world and return to the Father, in the course of a meal he washed their feet and gave them the commandment of love. In order to leave them a pledge of his love, in order never to depart from his own and to make them sharers in his Passover, he instituted the Eucharist as the memorial of his death and Resurrection, and commanded his apostles to celebrate it until his return; "thereby he constituted them priests of the New Testament." (337, no. 1337)

On the sacrificial character of the Eucharist, the *Catechism* notes what is a common accord among Christian churches, that the Eucharist is a sacrifice of praise and thanksgiving and is "the memorial of Christ's Passover, the making present and the sacramental offering of his unique sacrifice, in the liturgy of the Church which is his Body" (343, no. 1362). Specific Catholic tradition, however, affirms that the sacrament is itself a sacrifice because it represents (makes present) the sacrifice of the cross, of which it is the memorial and because it applies its fruit of this sacrifice. However, the sacrifice of the cross and the sacrifice of the Eucharist are one single sacrifice. This is the sacrifice of the Church, because in it the Church participates in the sacrifice of her Head, and she herself is offered in this offering, unites herself in it to Christ's intercession to the Father "for all men," and offers it for the living and the dead (344, no. 1368).

On the presence of Christ in the Eucharist, under the forms of bread and wine, the Vatican Council and the *Catechism* begin by recalling the many presences of Christ. The *Catechism* elaborates more fully on this matter by pointing to Christ's presence in the Word proclaimed, in the Church's prayer, and in the poor, the sick, and the imprisoned. To these it relates the unique and special presence in the sacrament. Here Catholic teaching constantly recalls the formulation of the Council of Trent: in the sacrament, "the body and blood, together with the soul and divinity, of Our Lord Jesus Christ and, therefore, the whole Christ is truly, really and substantially contained." Furthermore,

> because Christ our Redeemer said that it was truly his body that he was offering under the species of bread, it has always been the conviction of the Church of God, and this holy council now declares again, that by the consecration of the bread and wine there takes place a change of the whole substance of the bread into the substance of the body of Christ our Lord and of the whole substance of the wine into the substance of his blood. This change the holy Catholic Church has fittingly and properly called transubstantiation. [1]

Recent dialogues between Lutheran, Reformed, and Catholic Churches suggest that the positions of these confessions on the manner of Christ's presence are not diametrically opposed, though they do differ, and that the differences do not warrant the anathemas pronounced in the sixteenth century. This conclusion is reached on the basis of a biblical foundation, commonly accepted, and on a better understanding of the historical disputes.

It is, however, because of the teaching formulated at the Council of Trent that the Catholic Church upholds the continued presence of Christ under the sacramental species even after the celebration is concluded and eucharistic elements are left remaining. On this ground, it authorizes Communion to the sick and promotes eucharistic devotions outside Mass. Attention to the form of these devotions in recent decades advocates that they be clearly related to the eucharistic celebration and sees them as ways of promoting the sense of the presence of Christ in the Church and in the world and of fostering a more active participation in the eucharistic action and Communion.

Other points frequently noted in recent Catholic teaching are the following: First, a commitment to the poor is expressed through communion with the Body and Blood of Christ and should be a pronounced feature of a community that makes the Eucharist central to its life as a Church. Second, some recognition is given to the Eucharist as celebrated in other churches, but no commonly accepted doctrinal and canonical expression on this has yet been constructed. Within the mutual recognition of one Baptism, and with the respect given to each other's celebration of the sacramental memorial of Christ's sacrifice, it is the true hope and desire of the Catholic Church that churches will work together toward the one celebration of the Eucharist and the sharing of a common eucharistic Table.

Sharing the Communion Table

The Reformed Churches and the Catholic Church have different polities on the admission of members of other churches when they are present at a celebration of the Eucharist.[2] On the Catholic side, there was and still is some difficulty in recognizing the ordained ministry in other churches and thus pronouncing on the validity of the eucharistic celebration. When celebration is done in a manner that is consonant with the eucharistic tradition of the Catholic Church, the Church sees in it a memorial of the sacrifice of Christ, in which Christ and the Spirit are present and active. However, the

Church has not yet worked out a position on the precise sacramental nature of this celebration, given remaining questions about the validity of any ordination that is not done within the unbroken, historical episcopal tradition of the laying-on of hands.[3] Further, even if the Catholic Church were to recognize the ordination of the Churches of the Reformation as valid, this would still not be taken as a sufficient warrant for sharing the eucharistic Table or for the practice of an open Table.

In its ecumenical directives, the Catholic Church enunciates two principles that must govern admission to the eucharistic Table of the baptized of other churches and the accession to their Table by Catholics. The first is that a mutually recognized Baptism and agreement on the confession of eucharistic doctrine provide some ground for sharing the sacrament. The second principle, however, is that eucharistic celebration and eucharistic Communion must be done within a concrete gathering of Christians, united in all other aspects of church life, both doctrinal and institutional. Hence, normally, admission to the eucharistic Table is granted by the Catholic Church only to the members of those churches who profess and practice communion with the Church and the Bishop of Rome. A shared Eucharist is not taken as a means towards unity but as its apex and full expression.

On the basis of the first principle, however, which is the mutual recognition of Baptism, some exceptions to the normal ruling are allowed when circumstances and the condition of the recipient of Communion warrant them. The Catholic Church allows its ministers to occasionally give Communion to members of other churches who hold a eucharistic doctrine that is consonant with Catholic teaching. This is done on special occasions, such as the marriage of two persons of different Churches and funerals when spiritual need can be most profound.[4] It can also be done in unusual situations when, for a period of time, Christians of other churches have no ready access to eucharistic services in their own congregations and their desire for the Eucharist cannot be satisfied. Catholics, however, may not receive Communion in Reformed Churches for any of these reasons.

Current Reformed Understandings
of the Eucharist

Before we turn to the substance of this section, it is important to define two terms. First, the word *Reformed* refers to the Reformed/Presbyterian tradition that has its roots in Europe and Scotland in the mid-sixteenth century. Second, the term *Eucharist* refers to the sacrament of the Lord's Supper or Holy Communion, which is at the very heart of Reformed worship.

The French Confession of 1559 describes a Reformed understanding of the Eucharist in these words:

> We believe that God truly and effectively gives us what is represented in the Lord's Supper and in Baptism, and that the signs are united with the true possession and benefit of all they present. Thus, all who bring the receptacle of pure faith to the sacred table of Christ truly receive what the signs signify. The body and blood of Jesus Christ are food and drink for the soul just as bread and wine are nourishment for the body.[5]

It is clear in this article that faith is the hand that receives God's gracious gift in the sacrament. Huldrich Zwingli, a first-generation Swiss Reformer, emphasized the faith believers need to bring to the Table, while John Calvin later balanced this by focusing especially on the gift of Christ's presence that feeds our souls. It was the Reformers' understanding that this dual emphasis, on God's grace and on the receptive faith that permeates scripture, laid the foundation for worship in the early Church. Word and Supper are the center to the Church's worship. Regrettably, Zwingli divided sermon from Supper in his liturgical development, which has left the Reformed tradition impoverished. Calvin, on the other hand, argued strenuously for the biblical unity of Word and sacrament that has encouraged the more frequent celebration of the sacrament in the latter half of the twentieth century. Reformed worship, which has found its apex in the Word read and preached, has rediscovered Calvin's commitment to the idea that the Supper presents the very same Christ whom the preached word presents to feed the deepest hunger of our souls.

The Lord's Supper, in the words of the liturgy of the Reformed

Church in America, is "a feast of remembrance, communion and hope." The call to remembrance is inspired by the meal as participants give thanks for the once-for-all sacrifice of Christ on our behalf. The worshipping community is also called to enter into communion with each other and Christ through the sacrament. This communion, a mysterious gift of the Holy Spirit, feeds our souls as the Supper feeds our bodies. Finally, we come to the Table in hope as it represents for us an eschatological sign of God's kingdom growing up in our midst. The radical justice of God's new community finds a home at a meal where all the baptized find a place.

The Reformed tradition has understood worship as primarily a time and place where God acts. Thus the Eucharist is seen as the sacrament where the congregation eats and drinks together and the Holy Spirit feeds us with Christ's very life. It is the Spirit who provides the bridge between the sign and seal of the sacrament and the person of Christ. We have understood that as the body is fed so is the soul, through the power of the Holy Spirit. The mystery of *how* Christ is present is left in the hands of God through the work of the Spirit.[6]

The means by which the bread and cup are received varies from congregation to congregation. Many have adopted a Zwinglian (and Scottish) practice of remaining in their pews as they are served and as they eat together. Other congregations invite people forward to receive the elements, often by intinction. A few have kept a Dutch Reformed tradition, which places the congregation around a table in order to eat the sacred meal together.

Because the Reformed tradition has been careful not to identify the presence of Christ as being too closely tied to the elements themselves, the bread and cup are treated with great respect during the service and disposed of with dignity following the liturgy. Home Communion or Communion with those who are hospitalized or unable to attend is offered through the ordained offices of the church.

The Reformed tradition has practiced what is called "open Communion" when deciding who is invited to share in the sacrament. All who have been baptized are encouraged to eat and drink with the congregation. In respect for our Catholic brothers and sisters, however, who are forbidden to participate in Communion at the Eucharist outside their own tradition, Reformed folk should be careful not to enforce hospitality on them. At the same time, Catholics who are present when the invitation to the Table is issued should understand that this act of eucharistic hospitality reflects an essential element in Reformed ecclesiology, just as their inability to accept the invitation reflects an essential element in Catholic understanding.[7]

Ecumenical families will often find that the Eucharist is celebrated less frequently in Reformed congregations than in Catholic ones, but with the deepest commitment to its central role in worship. The highest point of the eucharistic liturgy is the repetition of the words of Jesus at the Last Supper and the Communion, which immediately follows. The Lord's Supper is understood both as a gracious action of God to feed us the very body and blood (life) of Christ through the power of the Spirit and the faithful action of the congregation to be ready to receive such a remarkable gift. Not only does the Table represent God's providential care, but it also stands as a prophetic symbol in a world of great hunger. The sharing of the Communion meal graphically reminds us that we are all equal before God and have failed to share the abundance of creation in a world of great need. Tragically, the division at the Table remains a judgment on a Church that Christ has prayed to be one. The Reformed tradition remains deeply committed to healing its divisions so that the various members of the one Body of Christ can again find themselves at the Table together.

Conclusion

Obviously, it will be difficult for interchurch families to cope with questions of eucharistic sharing. While presenting the understandings of the Churches in such a way that convergences in belief and practice may emerge, we have also attempted to explain how and why the disciplines diverge. In addition, we encourage interchurch families to join together in eucharistic worship to whatever extent is possible. In this way we hope to offer some help, guidance, and encouragement to those in this situation.

This concludes the main part of our reflections on the challenges and possibilities of being an "ecumenical family" in the Reformed and Roman Catholic traditions. The two appendices that follow address a variety of practical issues that may arise as well as present a glossary of terms used throughout the publication.

Our study began with a reference to Jesus' prayer that "all might be one" (John 17:11). Our prayer is that this publication may bring us a step or two closer to such unity. May those who use it be filled with the presence and power of Jesus' prayer, that they may lead the whole Church to a deeper experience of what it means to be one in Christ.

Appendix 1

Some Practical Issues

*I*n the course of their life together, an interchurch family has to face some practical issues on which its church traditions diverge. The aim of this appendix is to explain a number of these issues. After listing some resources for marriage preparation and the counseling of couples, it deals with family planning, the promises asked of a Catholic party to a marriage, and the meaning of dispensation and annulment in the current canon law of the Catholic Church. Given the nature of the questions concerned, the appendix lacks perfect coherence, but it is hoped that the matters set forth will be of assistance to couples, their families, and their pastors.

Resources for Couple Counseling and Marriage Preparation

The Premarital Investigation (PMI)[1] and/or FOCCUS (Facilitating Open Couple Communication, Understanding, and Study)[2] are instruments used in the Catholic Church for assisting the couple in understanding each other as distinct individuals who are willing to find ways to bridge differences and to find strength in what they have in common. They may also reveal whether or not the couple has the capacity to enter into a permanent marriage.

After responding to each of the questions in the PMI or FOCCUS, the couple reviews the results with a priest, deacon, or married couple trained to help those who are engaged. They explore those areas where the couple needs to learn to communicate better, discuss issues they have not yet clearly faced as a couple, and engage those areas where they disagree so that these don't become obstacles to a healthy marriage.

Some of the issues presented to the couple in the FOCCUS are life styles, mutual and separate friends and interests, ways in which their personalities complement and match each other, communication skills, parenting decisions, issues of sexuality, and other concerns that face every married couple. The instrument recommends a series of books and articles that could assist the couple as well as those who minister with them.

The section of FOCCUS on "Interfaith Marriages" urges the engaged couple to face conflicts that may arise regarding religious belief or practice and openness to having children and to consider ways the family can grow together despite differences that they might have.

Family Planning

For both Catholic and Reformed Christians, the realms of sexual morality, conjugal chastity, and family planning are directed by conscience that is well formed in the light of God's word.[3] Family planning is an area in which the Catholic position on authority in the Church makes special demands of the Catholic partner. The Catholic understanding of the Word of God embraces tradition as well as scripture and is subject to the guidance of the Church's teaching authority. The Catholic spouse in an interchurch couple is therefore obligated to form his/her conscience in light of church teaching. In the realm of marital relations this includes openness to having children.

The Catholic Church encourages a proper regulation of the size of a family in keeping with the means of each couple and the demands of life in society. However, in planning a family and limiting births, a couple is not permitted any artificial means that enter into the act of sexual intercourse, though it is permitted to limit the act to periods of expected infertility when necessary. The Church also forbids the use of infertilization methods that do not respect the integrity of the act of sexual intercourse. Thus in regulating the number of children, a couple must not use contraceptives, artificial insemination, or any other form of fertilization that is not consonant with the normal act of sexual intercourse.

Guided by prayer, by God's word in scripture, by the inspiration of the Holy Spirit, and on occasion by the advice of others, Reformed Christians share with Catholics the formation and education of conscience. Reformed Christians, while encouraging an openness to children under appropriate circumstances, do not intrinsically link sexual relations in marriage to procreation. In family planning they allow the use of the various legal means and technologies available. Artificial contraception is permitted, and the use of medical technology both in pregnancy prevention and conception is left to the dictates of the conscience of the couple.

Although neither tradition envisions abortion as a means of family planning, the question sometimes arises and is approached differently by each tradition. Catholic teaching considers abortion as the taking of a human life and therefore a grave violation of the commandment that prohibits this. (In other words, it is seen always as a sin.) While no Reformed tradition considers abortion to be the preferable option, there are no general ecclesial prohibitions on such a decision, and there are many differing views among Reformed Christians on the moral implications of abortion. This diversity is reflected in the official pronouncements of their Churches, and copies of these statements can be provided by their clergy.

In all these cases, the differences between the two traditions need to be approached by the couple in prayer and discernment, and with a strong and pure conscience.

Promises of the Catholic Partner

Catholic church law presumes that a Catholic will usually marry another Catholic. In countries that are substantially Catholic, this is normally the case. However, in pluralistic societies such as the United States, there is much intermarriage among Christians of various denominations. Frequently Catholics and Protestants fall in love and seek to be married in the Catholic Church or, with the permission of the bishop, in the church of the Protestant party.

The permission to marry a person of another faith tradition or to be married in a church other than a Catholic one is called a dispensation from the common provisions of the law.[4] In order for the bishop to grant this dispensation, the Catholic Church requires its own members to reaffirm their faith in Jesus Christ, to indicate that they intend to practice the Christian faith as a member of the Catholic Church, and to do all in their power to share their faith with their children by having them baptized and raised as Catholics. Before 1972 this promise was required by the Catholic Church not only of Catholics but also of the Protestants they were marrying as a condition for the granting of the dispensation.

In 1972 the Catholic Church's practice changed significantly in this regard. Although a promise is still required, it is to be made by the Catholic alone, and the Protestant[5] is simply to be informed of the Catholic spouse's promise. Further, the Catholic is to make the promise while taking into account the conscience of the Protestant party. The promise can be made orally or in writing. If the Catholic is unwilling or unable to make the promise, the bishop cannot grant the necessary dispensation.

The practical consequence of this change in Catholic discipline is that the promise of the Catholic is conditioned on the possibility that the Protestant may not agree to the Catholic Baptism of the children. For the sake of the marriage, the Catholic may find it necessary to agree to have the children baptized in the church of the Protestant spouse. It is essential that the question of the Baptism, as well as of the religious education and nurture of the children, be discussed carefully and fully by the couple before the marriage takes place, preferably with the counsel and assistance of their respective pastors.

Canon Law of the Catholic Church

The Catholic Church sees itself as both a divine and a human institution. Like all human institutions, it has laws that regulate major areas of its life.[6] The laws that govern church order and discipline, church structure, and church rules and procedures are called "canons" and are found in a collection or "code" called the Code of Canon Law.

The term *canon* comes from the Greek word for a measuring rod or ruler used by carpenters. Later it came to mean a standard of conduct. The Code of Canon Law lists the key standards or rules for certain areas of church life that express and protect the Catholic Church's beliefs and values. The Catholic Church believes that some of the most serious norms in its code are expressions of God's law or are essential to the nature of the Church. Others are disciplinary law or law created by the Catholic Church for good order.

For the most part, canon law applies only to Catholics. But when interchurch couples prepare to marry, they will find that canon law applies to them because it contains rules for Catholics about marriage and married life (canon 1059). The Code of Canon Law contains a basic description of the Catholic Church's teaching about the meaning of Christian marriage (canon 1055), including a list of the essential elements for marriage (canons 1056, 1057, and 1108). The Code also contains the requirement for marriage preparation (canon 1063), provisions about where Catholic marriages may be celebrated (canon 1118), rules about who may marry (1058), and a list of impediments, that is, things that prevent Catholics from marrying (canons 1083–1094). The Code of Canon Law also lists the basic rights and obligations of married couples in their relationship with each other and concerning the religious upbringing of their children (canons 1056–1058).

Couples are not expected to study canon law or to know all the rules and regulations. The pastor or people who help them with marriage preparation will explain the laws that apply to their situation and help them consider the options that canon law includes.

One of the unique elements of canon law is the provision for "dispensation." Sometimes the law imposes a hardship on a person or a couple that may not be necessary. If the law is a disciplinary one created by the Catholic Church, people can request a "dispensation." A dispensation is permission to set the law aside and not observe it in this particular case (canon 85). The diocesan bishop or someone he delegates is the person with the power to grant a dispensation. The Catholic Church will grant a dispensation from its disciplinary law when the value the law is meant to protect can still be achieved and when the dispensation will bring about something good for the person who requests it (canon 87).

For example, it is a Catholic church law that a Catholic must be married in a Catholic church, in the presence of a delegated Catholic witness (canon 1108 ff.). However, if the Catholic is marrying someone who is not a Catholic, the diocesan bishop can grant a dispensation from the law, allowing the Catholic to be married in the church of the other spouse as long as all diocesan requirements are met (canon 1127).

The Catholic Church
and Marriage Annulment

Because annulment, or a "declaration of nullity," by the Catholic Church is often misunderstood, we include here a further word of explanation.

The Catholic Church teaches that any valid marriage between two baptized people is a covenant, a contract, and a sacrament. While there is considered to be a *natural* bond between others who marry, the Catholic Church teaches that the marriage of two baptized Christians creates a permanent, exclusive, and indissoluble sacramental bond between the husband and wife. This bond cannot be dissolved for any reason except the death of one of the spouses. As long as it endures, the spouses are not able to enter into another valid sacramental marriage with anyone else.

A Catholic wishing to be free of a first union in order to marry again may ask the Catholic Church to investigate the first marriage to determine whether or not it was a valid sacramental marriage. This investigation is referred to as the "annulment process" and is carried out by a church tribunal, composed of people specially trained and appointed by the bishop.

The Catholic Church's judgment about the validity of a marriage is very different from a *civil* annulment. Those seeking a civil annulment are asking the state to declare that the marriage "never happened." This usually occurs very shortly after the wedding. When a couple asks the Catholic Church for a "declaration of nullity," the couple asks the Church to determine that what was in fact a valid *civil* marriage lacked the essential qualities to make it a valid *sacramental* marriage. The distinction between a civil annulment and a Catholic declaration of nullity is one that is often invisible in general discussion of the topic, and it is vitally important that families and their pastors understand the difference.

In making this kind of judgment, the Catholic Church considers the consent of the spouses and their capacity to carry out the obligations of marriage, and, if one of them is Catholic, it also looks at whether all the Catholic Church formalities were carried out. When two Protestants want a first marriage declared null so that one of them may be free to marry a Catholic, it is not necessary to inquire into the observance of church laws concerning the religious service.

For two people to enter what the Catholic Church considers a valid sacramental marriage, they must offer a free and knowledgeable consent to the essentials of marriage and have the basic capacity to fulfill the obligations of marriage. The Catholic Church teaches that the essentials of marriage are that marriage is a permanent union between a man and woman that involves the sharing of life, a faithful and exclusive sexual relationship, and an openness to have and educate children. This consent must be free; that is, the couple must choose marriage and each other without physical or psychological force. It must be knowledgeable in the sense that the parties understand and accept what the Catholic Church considers the basics of marriage. It must be true consent; the parties cannot exclude any of the essential elements (permanence, fidelity, or openness to children).

The second area the Catholic Church considers is the capacity of the parties to enter into marriage and to fulfill their promises. Sometimes people enter marriage in good faith yet lack the ability to live married life. They may be missing the basic psychological and emotional capacity to enter into a union of life and love and to form a real partnership with another person. This psychic incapacity may be due to a serious personality disorder or an untreated addiction that prevents healthy interpersonal relationships. One or both parties may lack the physical or psychic capacity for sexual intercourse.

Sometimes the limitations of the parties prevent a marriage relationship with a particular individual because they both lack the skills or have the same weaknesses and bring out the worst in each other. These issues must be serious in degree and must affect the essentials of marriage before the Catholic Church will judge that the parties are "incapable."

In cases where a civil divorce has already been granted, a person or couple may ask the Catholic Church to investigate the marriage. The formal request is submitted to a Catholic church tribunal. The tribunal personnel begin the investigation with the presumption that the marriage in question was valid and, if both parties were baptized, that a sacramental bond was created. That presumption can only be overturned by concrete evidence to the contrary.

In every investigation process both spouses are offered an advocate to help them. The former spouses are asked to give testimony about why they believe their marriage failed, to name witnesses who knew them well, and to present any other evidence that might affect the issue. When the investigation has been completed, all the material is studied and discussed by the tribunal personnel and a judgment is made. The case is then given to a second tribunal for study and review. When two tribunals have judged that something essential was missing from this marriage so that it was not a valid sacramental marriage, a declaration of nullity is given, and both parties are then free to enter into another marriage. If the two tribunals do not agree, a third tribunal reviews the case. If one or the other parties disagrees with the decision, provisions are made for an appeal of the case.

When a declaration of nullity is issued by the Catholic Church, it has no civil effects. It does not affect the civil status of their marriage, so it does not affect the legitimacy of their children. Both the state and the Catholic Church consider those children legitimate.

Nor does a declaration of nullity by the Catholic Church affect inheritance issues, custody of children, or other civil effects of marriage. There are also times when the tribunal judges that the marriage was a valid sacramental union. All married couples struggle and have difficult times in their married lives. At times these struggles, weaknesses, and even sin result in the death of a marriage relationship and a divorce. That does not mean that the marriage was invalid in the eyes of the church. Since the Catholic Church presumes that most people who marry have the basic maturity and capacity to live married life, the Catholic Church is cautious in issuing a declaration of nullity. When the tribunal judges that the previous marriage was a valid union, the Catholic Church says that the person is not free to enter into marriage with a Catholic.

If the couple then decides to marry before a Protestant minister or a civil official, the Catholic Church does not recognize that action as a sacramental marriage. While this lack of recognition is difficult for those involved, it represents the Catholic Church's fidelity to the teaching that Christian marriage is a permanent, faithful, and exclusive sacramental union that mirrors the relationship between Christ and the Church.

Appendix 2
Glossary

As our discussions progressed in this sixth round of the Presbyterian/Reformed-Catholic Consultation, it became clear to us that we would need a glossary. As we struggled with the intricacies of our Churches' understandings of the matters before us, we recognized that some of the terms we used represented language we hold in common. At times, however, each tradition uses terms distinctive to its understandings and practices. And we discovered that in some confusing circumstances, we use the same words but mean something quite different by them. Although this glossary is no doubt less complete than some might wish, it nevertheless attempts to reflect the language of faith as we used it and came to understand it in our dialogue.

Annulment (Catholic). In the Catholic Church, a declaration that something essential was missing from a marriage. While the marriage was civilly valid, it lacked one of the essentials to be recognized as a sacrament in the Catholic Church. This declaration has no civil effects, and it does not affect the status of the children, who are always considered legitimate. (See the fuller explanation in Appendix 1).

***Book of Confessions* (Presbyterian Church [U.S.A.]) (Reformed).** One half of the Constitution of the Presbyterian Church (U.S.A.), the other half of which is the *Book of Order*. The *Book of Confessions* contains eleven Reformed and Presbyterian confessions of faith, some of which are held in common with ecumenical Christianity and some of which are distinct to the Reformed tradition. They are the Apostles'

Creed; the Nicene Creed; the Second Helvetic Confession; the Scots Confession; the Heidelberg Catechism; the Westminster Confession of Faith; the Westminster Shorter Catechism; the Westminster Larger Catechism; the Barmen Declaration; the Confession of 1967, and A Brief Statement of Faith.

***Book of Order* (Presbyterian Church [U.S.A.]) (Reformed).** One half of the Constitution of the Presbyterian Church (U.S.A.), the other half of which is the *Book of Confessions.* The *Book of Order* consists of three parts: the Form of Government, the Rules of Discipline, and the Directory for Worship.

***Book of Worship* (United Church of Christ) (Reformed).** A liturgical resource for many occasions of public worship in local churches of the United Church of Christ.

Canon Law (Code of) (Catholic). The collection of 1752 laws or canons of the Latin Catholic Church that govern the general life of the Church and provide for good order. Most of these are disciplinary in nature. The latest edition was promulgated in 1983.

Catholic hierarchy (Catholic). The ordered structure of authority in the Catholic Church. The pope is the highest authority with jurisdiction or power over the whole Church. Bishops have authority over their local church or diocese. Priests have authority in their particular parish. There are other offices within the hierarchy that have a particular function and receive special honor. Cardinals are special advisors to the pope and are usually assigned to head offices in Rome or are in charge of major dioceses in a country. Archbishops are bishops in larger dioceses. Auxiliary bishops assist the diocesan bishop in a diocese. Monsignors are priests who have received the title as a special honor for service or work well done.

Civil marriage (Reformed/Catholic). A marriage witnessed by a civilly delegated/recognized official; one in which all the requirements of civil law have been observed; and one that has all the consequences of civil law.

Dispensation (Catholic). The Catholic Church's official action of setting aside the effects of canon law in a particular case. This requires a good reason, and the law must be one that the bishop or the one dispensing has the authority to dispense. The most common dispensations are given to allow a Catholic to marry an unbaptized person, or to allow the wedding of a Catholic and Protestant to take place in the Protestant's church. (See the fuller explanation in Appendix 1.)

Divorce (Reformed/Catholic). The dissolution of marriage under processes of civil law.

Ecclesial community (Catholic). The designation given in documents of the Second Vatican Council to the Churches that, in its view, lack full apostolic succession. This designation recognizes the ecclesial elements present in these bodies while at the same time indicating that they lack those elements that would give them full ecclesiastical status as visible manifestations of the Body of Christ.

Ecumenical directory (Catholic). The Catholic Church's *Directory for the Application of Principles and Norms on Ecumenism*. The current version was published in 1993. The directory contains rules or directives for situations of worship and shared activities between Catholics and members of other churches and religious traditions.

Ecumenical marriage (Reformed/Catholic). Another way of describing a marriage between two Christians who belong to different Churches.

Indissolubility (Catholic). The characteristic of a valid sacramental marriage. The marriage cannot be dissolved by the parties or any other authority as long as one of the spouses is alive. This characteristic prevents either party's marrying again until the death of the former spouse.

Interchurch marriage (Reformed/Catholic). A marriage between two Christians who belong to different Churches.

Interfaith marriage (Reformed/Catholic). A marriage in which the parties are of different faiths—for example, when a Christian is married to a Hindu or Muslim.

Liturgy (Reformed/Catholic). The public worship of the Church.

Local church (Catholic). The diocese of an area, under the leadership of and in communion with its bishop, made up of a number of parishes or congregations.

Local church (Reformed). The particular congregation or parish, along with those who are its members.

Magisterium (Catholic). The official teaching authority of the Catholic Church. Catholics are bound to follow the teaching of the magisterium in matters of faith and morals. There are different levels of this teaching authority, and Catholics are bound to different levels of adherence, based on the authority of the one who issues the teaching: the Pope alone, the pope and bishops in an ecumenical council, the Congregations or Offices of the Holy See (like the Congregation for the Doctrine of the Faith), and the diocesan bishop for his diocese.

Natural bond (Catholic). The Catholic Church teaches that a natural bond is created by the valid marriage within which one or both people are unbaptized. This bond can be dissolved either by a subsequent sacramental marriage or a dissolution (called a "privilege of the faith") granted by the pope so that one of the parties can enter into a sacramental marriage.

Nullity (Catholic). The declaration by the Catholic Church that an essential element was missing in a marriage so that it wasn't valid—that is, the sacrament effects did not take place.

Orthodox Churches (Reformed/Catholic). Eastern Christian Churches in communion with the Patriarch of Constantinople. One in faith and liturgy, they are known primarily by their ethnic or language identities, such as Greek Orthodox or Russian Orthodox. Their faith is set forth in the Nicene-Constantinopolian Creed. There are also Oriental Orthodox Churches that do not accept the Council of Calcedon and are not in communion with the Patriarch of Constantinople. Eastern and Oriental Orthodox Churches are not in communion with either the Catholic or the Reformed Churches.

Paschal mystery (Reformed/Catholic). The term used to describe the events by which one is saved—the passion, death, and resurrection of Jesus Christ and his reunion with the Father.

Piety (Reformed). Denotes those qualities and exercises of Christian life that commonly are characterized today as "spirituality." It includes a variety of experiences of personal devotional and corporate worship but is distinctly understood by Reformed Christians as relating experiences of grace and salvation to social relationships in the Church, community, and world. Piety is expressed by praying, reading the scriptures, singing hymns, practicing quiet meditation, and doing service in the world.

Reformed Churches (Reformed). A family of Christian churches emerging in Switzerland, France, Germany, and Holland during the last half of the sixteenth century under the guidance of second-generation Reformers such as John Knox, John Calvin, Heinrich Bullinger, Martin Bucer, and others.

Sacrament (Reformed/Catholic). A means of grace that by the Holy Spirit nourishes believers; a sign and seal of God's promise of salvation made effective by God's Spirit. In the Reformed Churches there are two sacraments: Baptism and the Lord's Supper (Eucharist). In the Catholic tradition there are seven: Baptism, Confirmation, Eucharist, Penance, Anointing of the Sick, Matrimony, and Holy Orders. There is also a "sacramental principle" in the life of faith that witnesses to God's interaction with God's people in the world. Catholic and Reformed teaching differs as to whether a sacrament actually conveys what it signifies. We agree that the sacraments are visible signs of an invisible grace and that sacraments offer grace and the faith to receive it.

Sacramental bond (Catholic). The Catholic Church teaches that an indissoluble [undissolvable] bond is created by the valid marriage of any two baptized people. This bond endures until death and prevents the parties from entering into a marriage with someone else.

Sacramental marriage (Catholic). The Catholic Church considers any valid marriage between two baptized people (whether Protestant, Catholic, or Orthodox) a sacramental union.

Spirituality (Catholic). A term used by Catholics to refer to the discipline of living one's life in relation to God by attending to the inner workings of grace and the external means chosen to develop this relationship.

Tribunal (Catholic). In each Catholic diocese there is a tribunal or court consisting of a group of experts in canon law who review and offer judgments on marriage nullity cases and other areas in church law where people may appeal ecclesiastical decisions or bring cases for judgment. The tribunal has advocates (who help people prepare their cases), defenders (who defend the marriage bond), promoters of justice, and judges. Most tribunals handle only marriage cases, but they can be asked to judge situations where there are canonical trials (clergy malfeasance) or administrative issues (wrongful termination cases).

Valid marriage in the Catholic Church (Catholic). A marriage that has all the essential characteristics. Both parties have the capacity to marry and freely consent to marriage. (For Catholics is the additional requirement that marriage be celebrated in the presence of a priest or deacon who has jurisdiction.) The "capacity" requirement means the parties are capable of a lifelong, faithful union and there are no "impediments" that stand in the way (like a previous marriage or lack of sufficient age). The "consent" requirement means they have given consent freely to what the Church means by marriage and that they have not excluded any of the essentials—unity, permanence, fidelity, a sharing of life, and an openness to children.

Validity (Reformed/Catholic). That characteristic achieved when all the essentials are present for the effect to take place. Without these essential elements, something may appear to have happened but with no effect. For example, a "valid Baptism" occurs only when water is used and the trinitarian formula is spoken. In the absence of either element an act that otherwise "looks like" Baptism might occur but without sacramental effect.

Reformed/Catholic Ecumenical Consultation

Members of the Consultation Team

Cochairs

Most Reverend Patrick R. Cooney, Bishop of the Diocese of Gaylord, Gaylord, Michigan

The Reverend Dr. John C. Bush, Presbyterian Church (U.S.A.), Bloomfield Hills, Michigan

Catholic Members

Dr. Ralph Del Colle, Associate Professor of Theology, Marquette University, Milwaukee, Wisconsin

Reverend Monsignor Alan F. Detscher, St. Catherine of Siena Parish, Riverside, Connecticut

Sister Sheila O'Dea, Associate Director, North American Forum on the Catechumenate, Washington, D.C.

Reverend Dr. David Power, The Catholic University of America, Washington, D.C.

Sister Ann Rehrauer, President, Sisters of St. Francis of the Cross, Green Bay, Wisconsin

Reverend Juan J. Sosa, Pastor, St. Catherine of Siena Church, Miami, Florida; Executive Director of Worship and Spiritual Life, Archdiocese of Miami; and President, National Hispanic Institute of Liturgy

Reformed Members

The Reverend Dr. Gregg Mast, First Reformed Church (R.C.A.), Albany, New York

The Reverend Martha Murchison, Presbyterian Church (U.S.A.), Dallas, Texas

The Reverend Dr. Zaida Perez, United Church of Christ, Hispanic Theological Institute, Princeton, New Jersey

The Reverend Dr. Lydia Veliko, Ecumenical Officer, United Church of Christ, Chicago, Illinois

The Reverend Dr. Carol Bechtel, Reformed Church in America, Professor of Old Testament, Western Theological Seminary, Holland, Michigan

Observer

The Reverend Dr. Scott S. Ickert, Resurrection Lutheran Church (E.L.C.A.), Arlington, Virginia

Staff

Dr. Eugene Fisher, Secretariat for Ecumenical and Interreligious Affairs, U.S. Conference of Catholic Bishops, Washington, D.C.

The Reverend Dr. Douglass Fromm, Ecumenical Officer, Reformed Church in America, New York, New York

The Reverend Dr. John H. Thomas, President, United Church of Christ, Cleveland, Ohio

Dr. Eugene Turner, Former Associate Stated Clerk for Ecumenical and Governing Body Relations, Presbyterian Church (U.S.A.), Louisville, Kentucky

The Reverend Robina Winbush, Associated Stated Clerk for Ecumenical and Governing Body Relations, Presbyterian Church (U.S.A.), Louisville, Kentucky

Notes

CHAPTER 1: SHARING LIFE TOGETHER

1. John Paul II, *On the Family (Familiaris Consortio),* apostolic exhortation of The Role of the Christian Family in the Modern World (Washington, D.C.: United States Catholic Conference [USCC], 1981).
2. United Church of Christ, *Book of Worship* (New York, 1986), 323.
3. *On the Family,* no. 56.
4. See the section on family planning in Appendix 1.

CHAPTER 2: PASTORS AND CONGREGATIONS/PARISHES

1. For a good resource, see Pontifical Council for Promoting Christian Unity, *The Ecumenical Dimension in the Formation of Pastoral Workers* (Catholic News Service, 1998).
2. For a more extensive discussion of this topic, see chapter 3.
3. For a more extensive discussion of this topic, see chapter 4.
4. This may be found in *Growth in Agreement. Reports and Agreed Statements of Ecumenical Conversations on a World Level,* ed. Harding Meyer and Lukas Vischer (Geneva and New York: World Council of Churches and Paulist Press, 1984), 433–464.
5. For a more extensive discussion of this topic, see chapter 6.
6. For a more extensive discussion of this topic, see chapter 5.
7. Pontifical Council for Promoting Christian Unity, *Directory for the Application of Principles and Norms on Ecumenism* (Washington, D.C.: USCC, 1993).
8. Faith and Order Commission, *Baptism, Eucharist and Ministry,* Faith and Order Paper, no. 111 (Geneva: World Council of Churches, 1982).
9. See the Formula of Agreement in *An Invitation to Action,* The Lutheran-Reformed Dialogue, Series III, ed. James E. Andrews and Joseph A. Burgess (Philadelphia: Fortress Press, 1984), 61–73.
10. The fifth round of the Catholic-Reformed Dialogue prepared an excellent resource for parish education in this regard, and it is highly recommended for broad use and study in our churches. Their work

is available under the title *Laity in the Church and in the World. Resources for Ecumenical Dialogue* (Washington, D.C.: USCC, 1998).

11.   George Kilcourse, *Double Belonging. Interchurch Families and Christian Unity* (New York/Mahwah: Paulist Press, 1992).

CHAPTER 3: OUR COMMON BAPTISM

1.   *Towards a Common Understanding of the Church: Reformed/Catholic International Dialogue* (Geneva: World Alliance of Reformed Churches, 1991), 55.

2.   This fact was demonstrated over sixty years ago by H. Richard Niebuhr in *The Social Sources of Denominationalism* (New York: Meridian Books, 1957).

3.   Faith and Order Commission, *Baptism, Eucharist and Ministry,* II. D.6.

4.   Pontifical Council, *Directory,* 92.

5.   *Rite of Baptism for Children* (New York: Catholic Book Publishing Co., 1970), 7.

6.   Michael Root and Risto Saarinen, eds., *Baptism and the Unity of the Church* (Grand Rapids: Wm. B. Eerdmans Publishing Co., 1998), 17–18.

7.   Ibid., 35.

8.   Ibid., 16.

9.   United Church of Christ, *Book of Worship* (New York, 1986), 163.

10.   Pontifical Council, *Directory,* 96.

11.   Root and Saarinen, *Baptism,* 16.

12.   Eugene Brand, "Worship and the Ecumenical Movement," *The Ecumenical Review* (April, 1999): 192.

13.   Kilcourse, *Double Belonging,* 112.

14.   Root and Saarinen, *Baptism,* 36.

CHAPTER 4: THE CHURCH

1.   Second Vatican Council, *Constitution on the Church* (*Lumen Gentium*) (Washington, D.C.: USCC, 1964), no. 8. Second Vatican Council, *Constitution on the Church,* no. 1.

2.   More can be found in the *Constitution on the Church,* and in the *Catechism of the Catholic Church* 2d ed. (Washington, D.C.: USCC, 2000), nos. 748–1130.

3.   More can be found in the *Constitution on the Church,* and in the *Catechism of the Catholic Church,* nos. 748–1130.

CHAPTER 5: THE COVENANT OF MARRIAGE

1.   These two qualities are referred to as *permanence* and *fidelity.*

2.   This is known as "A Dispensation from the Form of Marriage."

3.   See Lutheran-Reformed-Catholic Conversations, "The Theology of Mar-
      riage and the Problem of Mixed Marriages" in *Growth in Agreement.*
      *Reports and Agreed Statements of Ecumenical Conversations on a World
      Level,* ed. Harding Meyer and Lukas Vischer (Geneva: WCC, and Ram-
      sey, N.J.: Paulist Press, 1984), 277–306.
4.   In *The Constitution of the Presbyterian Church (U.S.A.),* Part 1, *Book of
      Confessions* (Louisville, Ky.: Office of the General Assembly, Presbyter-
      ian Church (U.S.A.), 1999), C 6.137.
5.   Ibid., C 6.132.
6.   Ibid.
7.   See the *Catechism of the Catholic Church,* nos. 1601–1642.
8.   For a more extensive discussion of these, see Appendix 2: Glossary.

CHAPTER 6: THE EUCHARIST

1.   It should be pointed out here that the word "substance" does not mean
      chemical composition but refers to the philosophical concept of "sub-
      stance" as used in Aristotilian and Thomistic philosophy.
2.   See Pontifical Council, *Directory for the Application of Principles and
      Norms on Ecumenism,* Part IV, B.
3.   For a more extensive discussion of this topic, see chapter 4.
4.   Pontifical Council, *Directory,* no. 130.
5.   Article XXXVII; Philip Schaff, *Creeds of Christendom* III (Grand Rapids:
      Baker Book House, 1969).
6.   Formula of Agreement, 9
7.   This background is discussed in detail in chapter 4.

APPENDIX 1: SOME PRACTICAL ISSUES

1.   The PMI or Premarital Investigation is done by the pastor or other quali-
      fied staff person in the Catholic Church according to a form approved by
      the diocesan bishop.
2.   FOCCUS questionnaires can be obtained by telephoning 1-888-874-2684.
3.   On the Catholic position on the regulation of births, see *Catechism of the
      Catholic Church,* nos. 2368–2372.
4.   For a more extensive discussion of dispensations, see pp. 74–76 in this
      chapter.
5.   The term "Protestant" is used rather than "Reformed Christian" as else-
      where throughout the text in order to be clear that the issues discussed
      here apply to all Protestants, not simply to those in the Reformed
      tradition.
6.   We are not here speaking of liturgical laws, which are found in the
      approved liturgical books of the Church.